SHADOWCASTING

AN INTRODUCTION TO THE ART OF FLYFISHING

by

John Dietsch & Gary Hubbell

With hope that a fish may rise —

John Dietsch

Copyright © 1999 by:

Clinetop Press

Post Office Box 95
Carbondale, Colorado 81623
970-963-0696 • 970-984-3801

ISBN #: 1-893740-02-1

Dedication

This book is dedicated to our fathers,
Al Dietsch and Ralph Hubbell,
who taught us to fish.
We are forever grateful.

Acknowledgements

Many thanks to the dedicated people who have freely given of their time, talent and thoughts regarding this book. Rodi Quitiquit modeled for the inside drawings, Chris Leithem modeled for the cover photo, Drew Reid demonstrated fly tying for us, and Graham Frandson acted as a sounding board. The drawings were executed by Ted "Mustang" Relihan. They're all "good guys" as well as "good guides." Paul Jacobson, George Odier and Roy Palm have also been special influences in our guiding careers.

It is important to note that in John's essays about his behind-the-scenes work on *"A River Runs Through It"* ("The Flyfishing Stuntman," "The Old Man's Knot," "Firsts" and "The Shadow Cast") he could not acknowledge all the contributions from the individuals on the film's fishing crew. In particular, the following people deserve special acknowledgement: George Croonenberghs and John Bailey for their integral roles as consultants; Jerry Siem and Jason Borger, who provided the lion's share of on-camera doubling for the beautiful casting sequences; and finally, Joe Urbani and Bob Auger, whose knowledge of fisheries biology was instrumental to the success of the fishing scenes. Many of the techniques and insights in this book come from our work with these gifted fishermen while making *"The ESPN Fly Fishing School."*

We honor the producers of *"A River Runs Through It,"* Robert Redford and Patrick Markey, whose passion and focus created perhaps the greatest ode to flyfishing ever captured on film. Very special thanks go to John Kelly for permitting us to use his gorgeous pictures from the set of the movie. We also pay respect to Norman Maclean, a man we never met, but whose presence is still felt—and whose origination of the word "Shadowcasting" has created a lasting symbol in the world of flyfishing literature.

Michael Bonds and Bland Nesbit are responsible for the beautiful design and production of this book, and we thank them for their talents and dedication. Kevin Stubbs and Nick Schmitt did a wonderful job of proofreading and offering editing suggestions, and we thank Michael Kerner for giving the final "thumbs up" to the galleys.

Perhaps most importantly, we acknowledge our wives, Mollie and Doris, for putting up with our fishing and our writing. If you're lucky, maybe we'll bring home a keeper one of these days (but don't hold your breath)!

Foreword

"I stood on the reed bank
ear tuned to the line, listening
to the signals from the ones who lived
under the blue barrier,

...I learned that the earliest language
was not our syntax of chained pebbles

but liquid, made
by the first tribes, the fish
people."

—Margaret Atwood

an has pursued fish since shortly after emerging from our once shared primordial muck to walk upon dry land. That pursuit has usually relied upon instruction of one sort or another. As a toddler, I first learned to trout fish from my dad and my Uncle Arnold on the Ausable in lower Michigan. My grandfather and Uncle Jim, who fished the rugged drainages cascading out of the pristine hills of West Virginia, were equally adept with fly rods. But their preferred catch was smallmouth bass, lots of them, mostly lunkers caught at night under a full moon.

Ironically, I have not evolved into a particularly good fly-fisherman after these many years, but I'm certainly an avid one, learning a lot more about myself in the process of fishing than I ever have about fly patterns or hook sizes. My three-year-old son will now challenge me—much as I did my elders—while he learns to listen to Margaret Atwood's elusive "signals from the ones who live under the blue barrier."

John Dietsch and Gary Hubbell have put together a disarmingly straightforward how-to that will enlighten, explain and entertain regardless of your proficiency with a fly rod. While preparing to produce *A River Runs Through It*, I read as much as I could about the subject of fly-fishing. Norman Maclean, Jim Harrison, Ernest Hemingway, John Gierach and Tom McGuane all wrote eloquent prose about the esoterica of the sport that I enjoyed very much. However, most of the tutorials available on the topic made computer manuals appear Proustian by comparison. *Shadowcasting*, on the other hand, will pique your interest with its judicious balance of empirical data and amusing anecdotes.

John Dietsch and the distinguished group of professionals (John Bailey, Jerry Siem, George Croonenberghs, Joe Urbani, Bob Auger, and Jason Borger), who worked so successfully with him on *A River Runs Through It*, assured Robert Redford and me that Norman Maclean's very specific fly-fishing approach would be reverently presented in the movie. Dietsch and Hubbell, whose writings and photographs portray their longtime experience as Colorado fishing guides, bring a similar attention to detail in *Shadowcasting*. Reading it will make you a better fly-fisherman—especially if you don't have a dad, uncle, or grandfather to help you learn that "liquid language" that the fish people speak.

Patrick Markey
Livingston, Montana

Preface

by Gary Hubbell

I remember the first trout I caught on a fly rod like it was yesterday, though it was 23 years ago. It was at dusk, and a tall pine tree leaned over the rich-smelling river. I skidded a Muddler Minnow across a rippling little pool, and a greedy little 11-inch brown trout slurped it in. I was ecstatic, and my father was beside himself with pride, coaching me through the cast, the strike, and the process of playing and landing the fish.

My father had made me serve a harsh apprenticeship. He believed that small children had no business with a fly rod in their hands, so he made me sit on the bank and watch for five years before he finally let me cast a fly line at the ripe old age of 11.

I had caught hundreds and hundreds of trout on spinning gear before that moment. I spent practically every waking hour during my boyhood summers hucking spinners and lures in the deep pools and shallow margins of the Roaring Fork River. But this feeling was different. I was an instant convert. With that little trout on the line, it was simply more electric, more intimate, more thrilling than even the biggest fish I had caught on a spinning rod. I was, shall we say, hooked.

Those were golden times, with the rich smell of the living water in the evening air and the sound of wild fish slurping up the snelled flies we had bought at Kenny's Pharmacy. I remember it like it was yesterday.

You, too, will always remember your first trout on a fly rod. It is one of those experiences of a lifetime, a milestone in personal satisfaction. However, some of you may not have a father (or mother) to teach you to flyfish; you may be well past age 11; you may not have easy access to a river like I did. But realize this: if you go about it the right way, flyfishing can be the most peaceful and rewarding thing you do.

Over the last two and a half decades, flyfishing has never failed to move me. It has brought me to many remarkable memories: wonderful places, to clean rivers, interesting people, funny situations, and some of my deepest friendships. It is through a common interest in flyfishing that John Dietsch and I know each other, and our collaboration on this book is the result of that friendship. From our many days of teaching people to flyfish on the Roaring Fork River, we've developed a method of teaching that we feel is among the best in the world.

Countless times we've heard, "Gosh, I wish I could find a good book on learning to flyfish." Well, now you have it. We will stress one thing throughout this book: flyfishing is not a contest. It is not about ego. It isn't your chance to show the world how good you are. Rather, it is about the doe and her fawn crossing the river, the osprey sitting in the cottonwood, the bluebirds eating berries on the bank.

Of course, you'll encounter your problems on the river. Maybe your waders will leak, or your knots will break when you get a big fish on. Maybe you just can't master the cast, or your line will tangle. But I promise that your problems will be confined to fishing. You won't be thinking about the problem at work or the situation in Bosnia, and you won't be worried about how to clean up your credit-card bill. You'll just be fishing.

Realize that this book is our attempt to teach you to do it right. If you follow the basics outlined in this book, not only will you be a pretty fair fisherman, but you'll also be a friend of rivers and trout everywhere. You'll remember it all your life.

Introduction

by John Dietsch

"In our family there was no clear line between religion and flyfishing...all good things, trout as well as eternal salvation, came by grace and grace comes by art and art does not come easy."

—Norman Maclean
A River Runs Through It

Flyfishing is not about catching fish, nor is it solely about spiritual renewal. Ours is a many-faceted sport that involves a unique understanding of nature and a willingness to listen to the river. The soul of flyfishing lies at the bottom of every riverbed, to be renewed again and again, each time we set foot in the stream.

It is my belief that we are able to come closest to understanding the "religion" of flyfishing when our performance on the river becomes second nature. By becoming a better flyfisher, we are able to better immerse ourselves in the river and to find the true soul of the sport.

In this book, Gary and I share our decades of flyfishing knowledge to help you become more intimate with the waters that we love so well. In 1991 I had the good fortune to work as the flyfishing production coordinator on the film *"A River Runs Through It,"* which was one of the defining moments of my dual career as a filmmaker and a flyfisherman. Before working on the film I was a guide in Aspen, and although I have continued to guide part-time since the filming of the movie, I have spent most of my summers on the rivers of Montana making commercials,

TV series, and videos that involve my most beloved sport.

There is no doubt that the film *"A River Runs Through It"* popularized the sport of flyfishing, and perhaps to excess. Some rivers are becoming crowded, and some have reached a point of saturation. This, too, will pass. In my mind, it cannot be a bad thing that more people have spent peaceful days on a trout stream. That simply means that there are more people who will stand up to defend our precious rivers when the next power plant, waste dump or strip mall threatens our trout streams.

In this book Gary and I have brought together many of the techniques and angling concepts from the folks I hired to help supervise the production of the fishing scenes from *"A River Runs Through It."* In addition we have borrowed from many of the guides, fishermen and mentors who have helped us to become the fishermen we are today. The information in this book is not highly scientific or technical. It's designed for the beginning to intermediate flyfisherman who wants to improve while being entertained. After all, isn't that what flyfishing is all about?

Table of Contents

Chapter One
The Big Picture

Flyfishing is a beautiful sport. That's why you've picked up this book. There are many attractive aspects to it. First, everyone loves water, and this is a sport that is very intimate with water. It's also a sport that is intimate with nature, and then, of course, it is the most peaceful of pastimes. You can spend hours on a river and your biggest concern may be your fly gets a little waterlogged and doesn't float as well as you'd like, but otherwise, all the concerns and worries of the big bad world out there just seem to melt away. And, admit it, flyfishing looks cool. When you look through a magazine and see a photo of some old guy standing hip-deep in a clear stream, casually looping a golden line through the air, you think, "Wow. That looks neat. I wish I could do that."

Sometimes it seems almost forgotten that the ultimate goal of the sport is to catch fish. There is such a mystical appeal to flyfishing, to that skillful act of looping that line through the air, that it seems almost an afterthought to catch fish. There's a lot of mystery surrounding flyfishing, and we like that. It's fun to be part of a fraternity that people are so curious about. But we've taught hundreds of beginners how to flyfish, and we don't mind sharing our secrets. We're getting pretty good at it, so we thought it would be easier to just write a book and set things down. That way you can catch up on your flyfishing when you're sitting on the airplane, or taking a break from work, or whenever you need to be somewhere else. As beautiful and mystical as flyfishing seems, however, there are real reasons for the things flyfishermen do, and there is a lot to be learned.

We're fond of telling beginners that you don't need to be able to stand hip-deep in a raging torrent, casting an entire fly line, to be a good flyfisherman. Instead, we think the best flyfishermen are those people who have the greatest power of observation. Think about that. The person who observes the world around him in the finest sense is that person who can link things together. That's the person who knows which fly to use, how to present it, and how to set the hook once the trout has taken it. So we're going to try to teach you to open your eyes and start noticing things.

If we are to begin to understand flyfishing for trout, we have to know about the big picture: water, insects and fish. First, trout are found in cold, clean water with lots of oxygen. They can tolerate water so cold that it freezes if it stands still, but water above 70 degrees can be deadly to trout. The preferred habitat is a clean river or lake with water ranging from 45 to 55 degrees. Trout are very sensitive to pollution, whether it is heavy metal contamination, pesticide runoff, siltation, sewage infiltration or fuel spills. (This is why trout are called an "indicator species"—if they're not doing well, the environment is in trouble.) Trout also need a high concentration of oxygen in the water they inhabit. That oxygen content may be a result of several factors—the water aerating from rolling over rocks and boulders, wave action, or plant emissions— but a stagnant pond won't hold many trout.

Secondly, trout feed primarily on insects, so insects must be present in good numbers to sustain a trout population. When we speak of insects, we're talking primarily about aquatic insects whose life cycles occur for the most part underwater where fish can feed on them.

Thirdly, trout need cover—a place to rest from the tugging pressure of the river's current and a place where they can feel secure from predators. In a river, that cover could be a slot of calm water downstream of a rock, a deep pool where the current is slow, or a stretch of calm water near the bank. If a stream is a chute of rapids with no breaks in the fast current, it won't hold many trout. In a lake, trout also need cover, like canyons, coves and brushpiles. Above all, however, the lake must be deep enough that it doesn't freeze over in winter and must hold enough oxygen for trout to survive year-round.

Insects

In order to understand flyfishing, you must understand insects. The popular misconception is that trout eat insects that somehow find their way to the water, such as a bumblebee, a housefly, or maybe a beetle. Those land-based insects, called "terrestrials," actually do supply a small percentage of a trout's diet, but not nearly enough to feed the trout population year-round. In actuality, trout feed primarily on aquatic insects which live in the river environment year-round. They are always present in the trout's ecosystem, so there's always something for trout to eat.

If you remember your ninth-grade biology class, you'll remember that there are four stages to an insect's development: the egg, the larva, the pupa and the adult. Everyone knows about butterflies. The egg is, of course, the egg; the larva is the caterpillar; the pupa is the cocoon; and the adult is the butterfly. Well, aquatic insects have very similar life cycles, except most of their lives occur underwater. Let's use the caddis as an example. Adult caddis look like the little millers that get in your lampshades. Typically, they have a tent-like pair of wings that folds along the back, and their antennae droop forward over their faces. Most often, caddis are about 3/8- to 1/2-inch in length and range in color from light tan to dark brown.

If you look closely at a river in the summertime, you'll often see caddis somewhere in the picture. Let's assume we see a caddis bumbling around above the surface of the river. It dips and drops and flutters on the surface. If there's a trout in the vicinity, this might be dangerous behavior. A fish could snatch this insect off the water. So why this behavior? What is he doing? Well, it's most likely not a he. It's probably a she—a female caddis laying her eggs on the surface of the river. Every time she drops onto the water, she's attempting to lay eggs. When she drops them, the eggs slowly sink to the bottom of the river, all the time being carried by the current, until they finally attach somewhere.

When a sac of eggs sinks to the bottom of the river, they attach to the sticks and stones there, and then they grow into larvae. Of course, the larvae need food, and that is supplied by the phytoplankton in the water. Just as plankton exist in the ocean, they exist in cold rivers in the mountains, and it's a plentiful food source for billions of insects. Over the next year, the caddis larvae grow bigger and bigger, and toward the end of that year, the larvae change into pupae. The pupae begin to take on the characteristics of adult insects, with wings and feet forming inside the case.

(Mind you, we're talking in general terms here. There are dozens of subspecies of caddis to be found in our own Roaring Fork River alone, and most trout streams will have caddis present in some form or another. To say they all mature and hatch in the same manner would be erroneous, but generally speaking, many forms of aquatic insects follow this model. It's safe to say that every flyfisherman who has reached competence in the sport has been forced to become a fair amateur entomologist.)

When everything is right—the temperature of the water, the time of year, the barometric pressure, the amount of sunlight, the time of day—the pupae will crack open underwater, and the fully developed winged insects will emerge, surrounded by a layer of gas bubbles that help it float. The new adult insects make their way to the surface of the river or lake, and when they reach the top of the water, they will generally spend a few moments drying their wings before flying off. This is a very vulnerable time for insects, so their safety is in numbers. Though the trout are slurping and the birds are gobbling, enough of the adults make it to the safety of the bushes and trees lining the river to mate. Once the female's eggs are fertilized, she drops them on the water and the process begins again.

Each species of insect is different, and their life spans and habits vary widely. But when we consider the insects involved in flyfishing, their life spans underwater are generally at least a year and sometimes as long as four years. Sometimes the adults may live as long as a month flying around near the river, but very often their adult phase is as short as half a day, or perhaps three or four days. The underwater phase is by far the longest part of an insect's life, and that's why it's such an important part of flyfishing. We call this underwater phase the "nymph phase" of an insect's development.

When you turn over a rock and see the critters crawling around on it, that's what you see—nymphs.

The Senses

The best way to understand how the life cycle works is to do as the fish do—get in it. Our goal as your teachers is to get you to open your eyes, to notice what's around you. Practically everyone has been near a river in his or her lifetime, but very few people really understand how they work—including quite a few flyfishermen. The next time you walk up to a stream, we encourage you to really observe it closely. Many things will be happening that you didn't see before. First of all, notice the color and temperature of the water. Is it clear? Murky? Warm? Cool? How does it smell? Rich and a little swampy? That's good. It means things are growing in there.

Next, walk in a few feet. Don't get yourself in any trouble, but get in far enough that there's a little current and you're at least ankle deep. If you don't have waders, you can stand it for a few minutes. Next, roll up a sleeve, reach into the water and pick up a rock. Find one about the size of a big grapefruit. Bring it out. Now look at it. Upon close inspection, the rock should start to "move," as the insects attached to it start writhing. If the river has much life at all, your rock will show you what the fish are eating. A typical rock in the Roaring Fork River, for example, will show you twenty or thirty tube-like shells about half an inch long. Those shells are manufactured from bits of leaves, twigs and tiny pieces of gravel to protect the caddis larvae inside. You might find a big bug up to 1½ inches long that looks like a fat scorpion. That's a stonefly nymph. Looking closer, you'll likely see some other scorpion-looking creatures with either a two- or three-pronged delicate tail. The mayfly nymphs you're looking at will range in size from a few millimeters to almost two inches long. The rock you've hauled out of the river might hold 50 or more insects. Just think—that's only one rock, and think of all the rocks right in front of you in the river! Trust us, the fish have plenty to eat. Most of the time when we escort beginning fishermen to the river, they have never imagined that a river could be teeming with such life. All we have to do is walk in and pick up a rock to see how a river works, but most people are never curious enough to do that. But let's go on.

The Big Four

Now we need to talk about the Big Four species of insects that are important to flyfishermen: caddis, mayflies, stoneflies and midges. We've already covered the caddis. Mayflies are the most beautiful of the aquatic insects, characterized by an upswept pair of wings that looks like a sail on a sailboat, a delicately arched posterior, and either two or three long, fine tails. They can range from a tiny size-20 "blue-winged olive" to an impressive inch-long, size 4 hexagenia.

Stoneflies are not very attractive insects. As nymphs they look fearsome, with menacing mouths and a long, armor-plated body. They look like they could bite you, but they're harmless. As adults, they have two pairs of wings that fold over each other the length of the body. They're slow, clumsy fliers. They're the biggest of the aquatic insects, growing to upwards of two inches in length on some Western rivers, and they're a favorite food source of trout.

Midges are, as the name sounds, the smallest of aquatic insects. If you pick up a stick lodged in the river and notice that it's covered by miniature little worms thinner than most fish hooks, those are midge larvae. While midges are tiny, they're an important food source for trout. Many subspecies of midges hatch in the winter, when trout don't have a lot to eat, so they provide an important winter food source. The adults are generally black or grey, and they look like those little bugs that get in the butter. On close inspection, you'll often see midges with fantastic antennae that look like sub-miniature clusters of ostrich feathers. Rarely are midges larger than a size 16 hook, and sometimes they're as small as a size 28, which is so tiny you can't even tie the fly on.

We talked about the caddis first because it, as well as the midge, conforms to what you learn in school about the four different phases of an insect's development: egg, larva, pupa and adult. But the mayfly and stonefly have only three phases to their development: egg, nymph and adult. Instead of producing a larva like a housefly or a caddis, the egg grows directly into a nymph, which looks the same throughout its growth until it hatches into an adult. Like a crab or a snake, its outer shell becomes too small as it grows, and the nymph cracks out of the old shell to enjoy its new large exoskeleton underneath. This process of shucking the old skin can happen 20 times or more as a nymph develops.

The Life Cycle

Now let's relate this life cycle to the fish. Insects are vulnerable to fish in all stages of their lives. Let's take a stonefly nymph. He is three years old and has grown to be quite large in the waters of the river. He's feeling the stirrings of his coming adulthood, and he's shifting around in the rocks under the river as he prepares to crawl towards the rocks of the bank. Suddenly there's a shift in the current and he's dislodged from his purchase on the rocks. He's swept downstream, and before he can wriggle his way back to the bottom, he's slurped up by a 16-inch German brown trout. Bye-bye. Actually, it's theorized that a trout's diet is comprised 90% of nymphs.

Let's look at scenario #2: a caddis is surrounded with gas bubbles and is emerging from its pupa case on the bottom of the river. It's halfway to the surface, and boom. A gorging rainbow trout adds our caddis to its menu. Then we have scenario #3. Other caddis manage to make it to the surface, where they dry their wings before taking off. The fluttering profile attracts a cutthroat trout that has keyed on the caddis hatch taking place. Slurp. Too slow, sucker. That was good. Think I'll try another. Gulp. But the fish can't eat them all, and by sheer numbers they manage to make it to the surface and fly away, where some of them fall prey to birds and lots of others meet fates like car windshields. But enough survive to reproduce.

We still have scenario #4. If you watch a river long enough, one day you'll see elegant mayfly spinners dancing above the water. Spinners are the final life phase of mayflies, whereby the adults that have emerged from the water transform themselves yet one more time before mating. They crawl out of their shuck and fly away a different insect. After the spinners mate and lay their eggs, they fall spent and dying on the surface of the water, where the fish make yet another meal of them.

Hatches

These cycles go round and round, year after year, season after season. In fact, each river will have its own schedule. For example, you could name half a dozen popular flyfishing streams that have a good Green Drake hatch, which is a fat, juicy mayfly that trout particularly love. A stream in Pennsylvania could be red-hot for Green Drake action in May, while a river in Colorado could be just beginning its Green Drake hatch in July. The rhythm of a hatch could be radically different in just a few miles of river. For example, the Frying Pan River flows into the Roaring Fork River at Basalt, Colorado. The Green Drake hatch is active on the Frying Pan right in the middle of the afternoon—say 1:00 to 3:00—through August. But on the Roaring Fork, just a few miles downstream, the action happens in early July, right at dark.

On a given stretch of river, a hatch may last three days or as long as a couple of months, depending on the river and the insect. On one river, there may be dozens of different hatches over the course of the year, several of them occurring simultaneously. Though beginning flyfishermen are concerned primarily with only four types of aquatic insects—mayflies, caddis, stoneflies and midges—each species is represented many times. An entomologist once told us that just in the 70-mile stretch of the Roaring Fork and Colorado Rivers from Rifle to Aspen, there are 57 different subspecies of caddis, each with its own peculiar lifespan and rhythm.

Imitations

Now let's relate that to the flyfisherman. (Note: We won't attempt to be politically correct throughout this volume. We find the term "flyfisherperson" clumsy and awkward, and "flyfisher" lacks something. We welcome men, women, and children of all races, creeds and backgrounds to the water, as long as they practice catch and release, show good etiquette, don't whine, and don't litter. "Flyfisherman" means anyone with a fly rod in his or her hand.) The way we catch fish is by imitating the insects that are present in the water. We do this by tying an artificial imitation of that insect onto a hook. The materials are usually natural, like rabbit fur, calf's tail, rooster's feathers, goose quill, or a squirrel's tail. The goal is to make the artificial fly look as much like the natural insect as possible, then present it to the fish and fool him into eating it. When he eats it, (or "strikes", in fishing parlance), the fisherman sets the hook, plays the fish into the net, and then hopefully releases it unharmed for another angler or another day.

That sounds pretty simple, and it is. Before you get too caught up in knowing all the names of the flies (which are many and extremely various) and the insects (which are often in Latin and therefore doubly confusing), all you need to know is this: the fish are eating a bug. Do I have one that looks like it in my fly box? If so, let's tie on that fly and throw it out there.

Observation

This is where the power of observation is especially important. It really is an intellectual pursuit. Here's an example. August is often slow fishing on our rivers, because the water is warm, many of the insects have already hatched out, and the fish are full, fat, and sluggish. It takes a good fisherman to catch fish under those conditions. Yet one day we watched our guiding partner, Paul Jacobson, nail fish after fish by casting to very shallow water right next to the banks, using a very large, bright orange caddis imitation. It would never have occurred to us to do what Paul was doing, but he was very successful. He explained, "Well, I've noticed this big orange caddis, but I've never seen any of them emerging from the middle of the river. I always see them on the rocks on the bank. So I figured they must crawl out to the banks to hatch like a stonefly, and the fish have to wait in the shallow water if they're ever going to get a crack at them." Indeed. Since that day Paul's observation has helped us through many dog days in August.

Through observing the happenings on the river, we can determine how we fish. When you first step onto a river, there are indicators as to the insect activity. Trout are opportunistic—they take what comes their way. Trout are also the classic calorie counters. They must gain more energy in the act of feeding than they expend. If there is a very active hatch of big insects in strong, fast water, you'll find fish there, because there is a net calorie gain for the fish to feed there. If a trout can gain more calories by feeding than they lose by working for them, then they will feed. If there isn't a great deal of insect activity, the trout will lay low and sip up the occasional nymph that drifts by.

So you approach a river with rod in hand and you wonder how to fish it. Well, by now we know that fish feed both below the surface and on the surface. The first question is, do you see any insects on the water or in the air? Second, do you see any fish jumping ("rising" in fisherman's vocabulary)? If you observe insects struggling to fly away from the surface of the water, and especially if you see fish rising to eat them, then it's a good idea to try a dry fly. Fishing a dry fly means you are casting a fly that's designed to float on the surface of the river and imitate the hatching insects.

If there's no activity on the surface, then it's a good idea to try fishing a nymph. That means you're imitating the immature forms of the insects that live below the surface of the river and to do so, it normally requires a certain amount of weight on the line to sink the fly to the level of the fish.

Style

There is a definite difference in style between nymphing and dry fly fishing. Dry fly fishing is considered to be the more elegant of the two forms. It's more graceful to cast a line without weight on it, and it's very exciting to see the trout rise to take the fly. Nymphing is more direct—let's say down and dirty—and there are more than a few purists who simply refuse to nymph. It is, however, extremely effective, although casting is hindered somewhat by the weight on the line and you're forced to detect strikes by markers on the leader called strike indicators.

Being able to catch fish on a dry fly is not always a given. There are just some days and some rivers where you won't raise a thing. You can go through your fly box and throw the book at 'em, and sometimes you won't catch fish. But it is a rare day indeed when a good nymph fisherman gets skunked. Personally, we go through periods when we would rather fish nymphs than dry flies, and other times we'd rather cast a dry fly than a nymph. It's always fun to catch fish, however, and we're like many other fishermen—we do what works at the time.

The Power of Observation

by Gary Hubbell

Paul Jacobson is perhaps the finest flyfisherman I know. Sure, there are guys who can cast farther, or guys who know more Latin names for insects, and there are certainly guys who are better fly tyers, but as an all-around flyfisherman, Paul gets my vote as the best.

The one factor that makes Paul stand out above the rest is his power of observation. I'm very fond of telling my guiding clients that the best flyfisherman is not that person who can stand hip-deep in a raging torrent and cast an entire fly line; it's that person who has the greatest power of observation. And every time I say that, I'm thinking of Paul.

For several years, I badgered him to join me on an elk hunt or a grouse hunt, knowing that he would enjoy those beautiful days afield. He desisted, preferring to spend his days on the trout streams. Once he joined me at my game, however, he quickly became better than I at tracking elk or finding the elusive blue grouse. He'd tell me, "You know, I saw a place yesterday that looks good for grouse. It's about 10,000 feet in elevation, with south-facing slopes, and a stream running through the basin, and lots of currant bushes. Grasshoppers all over the place. The grouse have to be there." And he'd be right.

Other days, he'd make an observation like "You know, I've never seen many grouse on granitic soils. I think they like limestone a lot better. Maybe the calcium builds better eggshells for hatching the clutch of eggs."

While the statewide success rate for elk hunters stood at barely better than 20%, Paul went out his first four years in a row and shot a nice elk. He is challenged by elk hunting, but he doesn't think it's particularly hard. "All you have to do is get out and walk and open your eyes," he says.

As a fly tyer, one of Paul's special creations is called the "Jake's Drake." Paul noticed that trout sometimes refuse a normal Green

Drake pattern, and theorized that the fly wasn't moving like a natural insect would. So he devised a pattern with unusually long wings—over two inches long—that skitters on the water when a puff of breeze meets the water. From beneath the surface, of course, the trout can't see that the wings are too long. They see only that skittering action, and WHAM! They can't resist.

One evening Paul and I were out fishing when I was working up an inter-connected series of pools. Oftentimes one or the other of us will fish while the other watches, and on this evening, Paul was the observer and I was the fisherman. The pools had little surrounding vegetation—only tall grass lined the ponds. A good caddis hatch was in full boil, and the trout were active. The pools were deep and slow, and in each pool I hooked a trout or two before the others became too spooked by the thrashing of the fighting trout. The fish were uniform German browns, all twelve- or thirteen-inchers.

In one pool there was a solitary river birch overhanging the water, and a nice trout was rising steadily under the bush. I cast to him, the trout rose, and I set the hook. It was obvious from that moment that the trout was bigger than all the others. As I played him into the net, Paul commented, "You know why that trout was bigger than all the rest, don't you?"

I hadn't given it a thought. "No, why?" I replied.

"Well, look at where you hooked him. Right under the birch, right?"

"Well, yeah..." I said hesitantly.

"Ants like birch trees, right? That means he's got a food source that none of the other trout have. If you came back here during the heat of the day and flipped an ant pattern under that birch, I promise you, you'd hook that fish again. The reason he's so much bigger than the rest of the fish is that he's sitting there all day slurping up ants that are falling off that birch tree."

"Oh," I said, humbled. "Sounds good to me."

Chapter Two
Casting
and Presentation

Ah, fly casting. Now that we're past the analytical part, let's wax poetic. For a flyfisherman, nothing is more beautiful than casting a looping line through the morning mist above a clear stream. It is peace and justice and serenity. It is zen. When novices see a photograph or a film clip of a flyfisherman, they automatically think of this graceful casting motion, and that's what they want to do. It's like watching Greg Norman hit a golf ball, or Michael Jordan slamming a dunk home. It's beautiful.

But some people are bewildered by fly casting. There's a fuzzy connection between this beautiful casting and actually catching fish. Some people think all you do all day is throw the line back and forth, and somehow in between, you catch fish. We've heard some interesting comments, like "Well, you throw the fly above the trout's head, and the third time he jumps out of the water and catches it, right?" Or, "Why do you keep throwing the line back and forth so many times?" That's actually a pretty valid question. But the best question we've ever heard was "How can you catch a fish when the line is always in the air?" Exactly. You can't.

Fly casting is like any other sport. The situation is always changing, never static. Motion is necessary. But let's start from the beginning. Initially, the reason for casting is simply to get enough line out to catch fish. Say a fisherman is casting to a trout 35 feet away. He can't cast the whole line at once, so he starts by stripping 15 feet of line out of his reel, then "false casts," feeding a few more feet at a time until he has enough line out to reach the fish. Then, when he realizes he's got enough line out, he may false cast, never touching the water, a few more times until he feels like he's got the range; then he finally casts for real, and lays the line on the water. That's what all that motion is about—simply getting the line out where he wants it. In its most efficient form, however, the caster throws the line only once.

Then, as the stream's current brings the line back to the fisherman, or perhaps the wind of the lake blows the line back to the shore, the fly caster finds himself with a bunch of line pooled around his feet. Then it's time to cast again, and he will false cast until he's got enough line out, and then he'll take a couple of range-finding casts, then he'll ultimately lay the line down on the water. That's what casting is about. Now here's how to do it.

Casting Basics

Before you even rig up the rod, find a nice, open space to practice. The back lawn, a city park, even a parking lot will work. Make sure there are no obstructions like low-hanging power lines, bushes, tree branches, etc. Place the reel in the reel seat so it sits on the bottom side of the rod and lock the reel seat. Run the fly line through the guides, and put a leader on the fly line. This leader will likely get trashed. Don't tie a fly on the line. It's unnecessary and even dangerous when you're learning. Instead, tie a little piece of bright yarn on the end of your leader. Strip some line out of the reel—no more than 20 or 25 feet to start with. Now you're ready to cast.

The first consideration in learning to fly cast is the grip. Like any other sport, fly casting demands the proper technique from the outset. Grasp the rod firmly, but keep the grip relaxed. In some ways, the motion of fly casting is like pounding a nail with a hammer. A good carpenter keeps his thumb aligned along the handle of the hammer, giving him control of the stroke. It's the same in flyfishing—place the thumb along the spine of the rod. Although many people think that fly casting is accomplished with a wrist action, it is not. Most of the power of the cast comes from the forearm, with a little "finish" with the wrist at the end of the stroke.

Secondly, there is an old adage in fly casting that "all fly casting

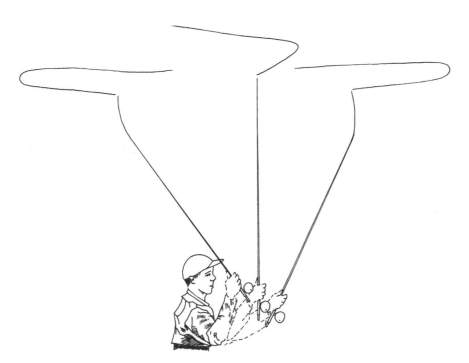

The "Ten to Two" rod position for dry fly casting

is done from ten to two." Imagine a fisherman's elbow as the center of a clock. He is facing to the left. The rod is the hand of the clock. When he casts, the rod should go no further forward than two o'clock. On the back cast, the rod should go no further back than ten o'clock. Actually, the image of a clock face is somewhat erroneous, because that gives the connotation that casting is accomplished in a circular motion. It's not. The fly rod does not prescribe an arc in the air like the hand of a clock. It goes forward and back, with the tip of the rod basically remaining at the same elevation.

As always, there are very good reasons for this. The goal is to throw the line forward, not down. If you bring the rod tip farther forward or back than ten and two o'clock, or if the rod tip makes an arc in the air, then the line goes down and puddles on itself, not forward.

Third, the fly caster must realize that the weight of the line itself is what makes it possible to cast. In spin casting, the lure provides the weight for the cast, and the motion is all forward. In fact, almost everything we do in other sports is all forward, whether it's hitting a golf ball, throwing a baseball, hitting a tennis serve, or casting a spinning lure. With fly casting, however, there are two segments of the cast, forward and back, and the back cast is just as important as the forward cast. On the back cast, the rod serves to "load up" the line in the air behind the fly caster so that he can cast it forward. This requires an equal amount of force for the back cast and the forward cast. When we're teaching beginners, we commonly encounter a syndrome where people cast very tentatively behind them, and very forcefully forward. It's very important that these two segments of the cast receive equal force.

Fourth, it's important to incorporate a pause into the stroke, right after the back cast and right after the forward cast. That allows the line to sail out in the air and, again, "load up" for the next cast. If there is no pause, the fisherman is simply waving the rod back and forth, and there will be no length to his cast.

To put it all together, if you watch a good fly caster, you'll notice that he brings the rod forward (not down in an arc) to ten o'clock, where he makes the rod tip stop. The rod is the catapult. When the rod tip stops, the line shoots forward. On the back cast, the fly caster brings the rod back with equal force to the forward cast, where, at one o'clock, he makes the rod tip stop again. The line "loads up" in the air behind him, and he's ready to throw it forward again. The longer the cast, the longer the pause between strokes.

Timing

When the rod is stopped in both the back and forward casts, it allows the line to form a loop off the rod tip. These loops, which look like a candy cane, are the main objective of the fly caster. The tighter the loop, the greater the ability of the line to slice through the air. A loose loop is a sloppy cast, and difficult to present to the fish. A loose loop usually results in a pileup of line on the water, which either spooks the fish or, if he takes the fly, allows him to spit out the hook before the fisherman can take up the slack in his line. Sometimes advanced fishermen use a loose loop for special presentations, but for now, try to cast a tight loop.

Many beginners think this casting motion takes tremendous

force. It doesn't. If you're a saltwater fisherman or a bass fisherman, you're going to have to tone down your macho "huck it out there" instinct by a factor of 10. It really takes very little effort to cast a fly line 30 or 40 feet, which is typically the longest you'll have to cast to trout on most streams. If you hear a popping or snapping sound when you're casting, that means you're exerting far too much force, and probably at the wrong times. It also means you will literally snap your leader when you're casting, and it's hard to catch fish without a fly on the line. Also, if your cast simply won't shoot out straight, but instead piles up on top of itself when you attempt to finish the cast, that means you're trying too hard. Tone down the forward part of the cast. Fly casting doesn't require much strength, but it does require timing, finesse, and skill.

We've spent some time working with Jerry Siem, acknowledged as one of the world's finest fly casters, and Jerry says that 90% of the casting motion takes place between the elbow and the wrist. You don't throw a fly line with your upper arm, like a baseball. You throw it with the rod tip. So if you're using your upper arm, shoulder, and biceps to throw a fly line, you're doing it wrong. Drop your elbow and tuck it into your side. Use the part of your arm between your elbow and wrist, and make the rod tip stop on the forward part of the cast, and on the back cast. Incorporate a pause both ways, and you'll be amazed at how the cast smoothes out.

Problems

Now let's talk about problems. If you cast forward and back in a straight overhand motion, at some point your line is going to tangle either on itself or the rod. It's important to keep the cast in the same plane, and to keep the cast rolling over the top of the rod. But if you're getting the line tangled around your rod, simply lean the rod to the side, about 15 degrees from vertical, and the line will travel outside the rod, saving you from tangles.

For women, who typically don't have the upper body and shoulder strength that most men have, it can become tiring to hold a rod and cast a fly line overhead for long periods of time. If a woman becomes overly tired from casting with her arm, we suggest that a woman use her source of power: her hips. Instead of throwing the line with her arm, she can simply tuck her elbow into her hip, and, never really using the arm for strength, she can rotate her hips to accomplish the throwing motion. It works.

Much can be accomplished to learn fly casting by simply practicing in the backyard or in the school playground. Once you're on the water, however, there are a few things you must know. First and foremost, you will not catch fish if you thrash the water with your fly line. Fish spook when the spray is flying from your line. If you are false casting, it is imperative to keep your line above the water. When you lay your line down on the water, the goal is to do it gently so as not to spook the fish. We have a saying: *"Spank equals spook."* Spank the water with the line and you'll spook the fish. Keep your line off the water when false casting, and when you lay the line on the water for a drift, do it gently.

Secondly, things are much different on a river, with the typical brushy banks, logs, rocks, rapids and other obstacles. These things make casting difficult. Take some time to inventory your situation. If you cast further to the right, is your back cast going to catch in that tree? How are you going to cast to that fish rising under those overhanging branches? Will your line get caught in that tangle of driftwood if you let it drift through that run? So while it's very valuable to learn to cast on dry land, you've got to do a whole lot more thinking when you're on the river. In the end, your cast may not even resemble what you learned on land, but as long as you present it to the fish, then the goal is accomplished.

Casting is full of old adages, and one of the most important is *"You can never cast a slack line."* Think about it. If you've got 35 feet of fly line puddled at your feet, there's no way you'll be able to cast it. Therefore, you must bring tension to your line before you can cast it. The easiest way is to simply shorten up. Pull in slack until you've got only 12 or 15 feet of line out, then lift up the rod tip, bring tension to the line, and cast. Once you've got the line moving, you can feed the slack into your cast two or three feet at a time.

Roll Casting

Sometimes you don't have the luxury of false casting, because perhaps you would tangle your line in the bushes behind you. Still, the line must be taut before it can be cast. To that end, fishermen have invented casts to get them out of tough spots. The best known is the roll cast. In situations where trees, bushes, or other obstacles make a back cast impossible, roll casting becomes essential. Roll casting can be described as a forward cast without the back cast. However, since the line needs energy to move it forward, the lack of a back cast has to be replaced with something. Essentially, a roll cast gains its energy from the fisherman slowly retrieving the line in front of him, lifting the rod tip to bring some tension to the line, then quickly (and powerfully) "rolling" the line forward.

The roll cast is not a pretty cast. It is simply functional. Some people get in the habit of using the roll cast almost exclusively, and that's probably because they've never really learned to cast a fly line the right way. When proper casting techniques are essential, like for distance or great accuracy, the roll cast will not be adequate. But if you need to get out of a tight spot, the roll cast will help you out.

Distance and Accuracy

Some fishermen think the ultimate in becoming a good fisherman is to make really long casts. We don't necessarily share this opinion. There is a difference between a "fly caster" and a "flyfisherman." From time to time, you'll find that there is no way to present your fly to a particular fish without making a long cast. But generally speaking, you're much better off if you simply move a little closer. Most fish won't spook if you use a little stealth and come within 30 or 40 feet, and sometimes you can catch them less than a rod's length away. A shorter cast gives you much more control, especially in the process of hooking and playing the fish. We are faithful believers in the principle of *"Don't cast more line than you can control."* When you're just learning to cast, 25 feet of line is a good plenty. As you progress, 40 feet is a very long cast. If you find you can't reach a fish with 30 feet of line, try to move closer.

In some fishing situations, you'll feel like a contortionist trying to get your fly to land where you want it. If, for example, there are overhanging branches with a trout rising underneath them, you may have to lean over to cast on the opposite side of your body (to avoid the branches overhead), then at the last second you'll find yourself slinging the line sidearm to slip it in the open slot. That's when you'll find yourself improving as a fly caster—when you're forced to make different casts for a variety of fishing situations.

It brings to mind a fellow that we guided several years ago. He had been flyfishing for a few years, and was getting pretty cocky about his skills. He was in good shape and had good basic technique, but had been fishing with a guide year after year on the same easy stretch of water. He told us he was ready for a challenge, so we took him to a particularly inaccessible stretch of the Roaring Fork where the wading is very difficult, the branches hang over the stream, the current is very swift in places, and the fish are concentrated in little pockets downstream of big boulders. In four hours of casting, our hero managed to hook one fish, which he didn't land. Not that he didn't have opportunities—there were fishing rising everywhere, and he missed more than a dozen hard strikes. He simply couldn't cast to them. We've guided fishermen who were skilled fly casters in the same place, and they hooked close to 30 fish apiece in an evening of fishing. After that evening on the Fork, he went home convinced he needed to really practice his casting.

By the same token, you shouldn't let situations intimidate you. If a piece of water looks difficult to fish, chances are it doesn't get fished very often, and you may have a great time there. Challenge yourself and improve your skills by fishing those tricky places, and you'll be rewarded by becoming a better fisherman. Remember the adages: "Ten to two," "Never cast a slack line," and "Never fish with more line than you can control." These dictums are so important that they can be crystallized into two simple words, the way that flyfishermen often conclude a letter to each other. Instead of "Sincerely yours," we write, *"Tight lines."*

The Shadow Cast

by John Dietsch

Perhaps the most memorable fishing sequence in the film "*A River Runs Through It*" is the Shadow Casting scene, a central metaphor in the film. Brad Pitt's character, Paul, stands alone in the middle of the Blackfoot River, water dripping off of him, and "he would cast hard and low upstream, skimming the water with his fly but never letting it touch." The theory was that Paul would create a "hatch" by zipping the fly along the water so many times that the fish would be compelled to eat it. I remember thinking that there is no "shadow cast" that exists in the lexicon of flyfishing.

It is a literary technique as much as it is a fly cast and it reminds me of trick roping at a rodeo—it looks cool, but for most cowboys it could never be used to catch a calf in the real world. As Norman wrote, "every fine fisherman has a few fancy stunts that work for him and for almost no one else." One of the key challenges on the film was to develop a cast and find a location on the river, on the perfect rock, that would work for everyone.

The saga of developing the Shadow Cast began in Los Angeles three months before we even started shooting the film. I first met Brad Pitt the day after he was hired to play the part of Paul, the great fisherman. As the flyfishing coordinator on the project, one of my jobs was to work with the principal actors—all three who had never cast a fly before—to teach them enough so they could pass for having flyfished all their lives. (We would also use doubles for the longer beauty shots.) Bradley showed up with a scruffy beard and funky sunglasses. I talked about flyfishing mostly as we drove to the local park in downtown Santa Monica. Back in those days he had yet to become the star that he is today.

Standing by the car we rigged up and then, finding an open grassy area, we began the casting lesson. He had never cast a fly rod before. I showed Bradley the way to hold the cork handle of the rod, with the thumb pointed down the top of the rod handle, and the hand centered between the butt of the rod and the reel. I pointed out that in fly casting, unlike spin fishing where a weighted lure propels the line in one quick motion, the weight of the fly line itself is what allows the flyfisher to rhythmically work line into the rod. I explained that the fly cast is based on the exact timing and technique of the strokes, back and forth from ten o'clock to two o'clock—ten to two, ten to two.

"Like the Reverend," Bradley pointed out, referring to the man who would be his father in the film, and who taught his son the basics of fly casting with the help of a metronome.

I explained the difference between the way the Macleans fished in Montana in the 1930's versus how we fish today (the biggest difference being that today's anglers use mostly fast-action graphite versus the slower-action of the heavy bamboo "Montague" or "Granger" rods used by most folks in Montana back then). I explained that casting with a slow action rod would usually require more ticks on the metronome during the same length of cast since the bamboo rod was a slower action.

Bradley picked up the casting as fast as anyone I had ever taught; it was obvious that he was a talent who could mimic actions quite easily. I had him switch between a bamboo rod and a graphite rod to see the difference between the casting actions, and as expected, he preferred the faster action of the graphite. He was amazed at the difference in the ease of casting between the two rods. I told him that we were in the process of working with an old friend of mine named Walton Powell—a veteran fly rod manufacturer—to adapt his slow-action graphite rods called "hexagraphs" into replicas of bamboo rods that the Macleans used.

After about an hour of instruction, Brad had the initial feel for casting. I picked up the rod and began doing a few unconventional casts. I began with a "reverse" cast. Instead of casting in the conventional style (for a right hander) with the rod casting over the right shoulder, I turned my wrist 45 degrees and cast (still moving from eleven to two) over the left shoulder. This reverse position, with the arm moving diagonally in front of my face, placed the cast 45 degrees to the right of center. By positioning the body 45 degrees to the left, the line then moved in the same direction of a standard cast, straight to center (I still use this technique when casting upstream on the right side of a river as I am looking up stream, especially if my backcast area is cramped by brush).

Then, trying to impress Brad even more, I added what is called a "pendulum" move to the backcast so the line came back fast and low just above the grass. Instead of stroking back high above me—like a normal backcast—I cocked the rod tip horizontally, so the line came back fast and low to the ground. I had practiced this many times along the rivers of Montana and Colorado when the fishing was slow and I was bored, and now I was simply showing off for this actor, hoping he would see what I saw in the cast, when suddenly he said, simply, definitively:

"The Shadow Cast."

Ultimately, in that moment, we created the cast for the film. (Norman had passed away, so it was up to us—and ultimately Redford—to decide what it would look like. Later, I would have several discussions with George Croonenberghs, who knew the Macleans and is mentioned in the book, who said that he had never seen the cast performed by Paul. John Bailey from Bailey's Fly Shop, and Jason Borger—who performed the stunt casting for the scene—would have input into the cast.) In the screenplay, the cast took on even more significance as it was the lasting visual that the narrator has of his brother in his element, far away from the trappings of civilization that would be his downfall.

The first day of scouting for the river scenes, including the shadow casting sequence, took place in one of the worst blizzards Montana had ever seen in April. It snowed three feet. No one else was driving on the highways, except for us. (I mean we did not see a single soul on the road!) The producer, Patrick Markey, picked up my friend Jim Belsey, a Bozeman local, and his associate, Joe Urbani, a fisheries biologist who ultimately became our trout wrangler. Both Belsey and Urbani thought we were crazy Californians for trying to scout flyfishing waters along the Gallatin River in April that would not be shot until August.

But as it turned out, when August came around, we spent several weeks shooting along the very section that those two characters led us to that miserable morning. I ended up scouting the section just above Squaw Creek bridge in the Gallatin Canyon three dozen times or more searching for the perfect rocks, eddies, and runs for each of the main fishing scenes–all of which were shot in that canyon.

In particular, I spent hours kayaking, hiking, fishing and wading in and around the Gallatin, throughout the canyon section, searching for the perfect rock from which to execute the "Shadow Cast."

So you can imagine my surprise when the time came to actually shoot the "Shadow Cast," and Redford decided to set up the scene just downstream from my "perfect rock" due to the light. Every time I look at the movie poster today, which shows the Paul Maclean character performing the cast from the "wrong rock," I am reminded of the hours I spent choosing an "imperfect rock." You can see it just to the left of where the actual character stands casting the line! Like a fishing trip where you end up catching fewer fish than you planned, the poster serves as a reminder to me of how some things in life may never work out the way you planned them, but they nonetheless work out just fine.

In the actual scene, I hid behind "Redford's rock" with either Brad Pitt or Jason Borger, who played Brad's casting double in the scene. Jason Borger–son of the famous flyfisherman Gary Borger–showed off his talents as a world-class fly caster as Brad and I hid behind the rock during "wide shots." Jason's slim profile and blond hair duplicated Brad's look perfectly.

In the tighter shots, Brad and Jason switched and Brad did a respectable job at line handling in tight closeups, imitating what Jason and I had choreographed as the cast.

Looking back, nearly a decade later, preparing, choreographing and shooting those fishing scenes were some of the most memorable days of my life.

Chapter Three
Dry Fly Fishing

Now that you know how to cast, you need to know how to actually catch a fish. If we go back to what we learned about the "big picture" in Chapter One, we recall the life cycle of the insects and the phase when they're hatching from the bottom of the river, emerging to the surface, floating for a few moments to dry their wings, and flying away. During such a hatch is the perfect time to fish with a dry fly.

That's when we tie on an artificial imitation of the insects that we see on the water and delicately present it to the fish. Dry fly fishing is everybody's favorite—it's exciting! The trout must rise to take the fly, and there's nothing like watching a fish come boiling to the surface to slurp in the fly that's tied to the end of your leader. Dry fly fishing is completely visual, in that you won't feel the fish take the fly; you'll see it. As with any aspect of flyfishing, it takes a fair amount of skill and technique to be good at fishing a dry fly, but a beginner can still catch fish.

There are lots of things to know about fishing a dry fly, so we'll go through them one by one. First, it's important to keep the fly on the surface of the water. There is no miracle fly that won't get wet and waterlogged after a period of time. When the fly sinks under the surface, not only is it impossible for a fisherman to see any strikes, but the fly is less appealing to the fish. So before we even cast a dry fly, we coat it with fly floatant, a product that keeps the fly floating longer. When it gets too wet, you can dry it with some powder.

Match the Hatch

Once you've decided to fish a dry fly, it's important to figure out which one you're going to tie on the line. There are hundreds and hundreds of flies, each with their own funky little name and reason for being, but they're all designed for one purpose: to catch fish. You don't need to know any Latin for entomological purposes; you don't need to even know the name of the fly you're using. You just need to know that it looks like the insects that the fish are eating. That's called "matching the hatch."

For example, you may be standing at streamside and you notice a trout rising. Every 15 or 20 seconds, he comes to the surface and splashes. He's doing that for a reason. Upon closer observation, you notice that there are insects floating on the water. They look small and grey, and as you look in the air and on the bushes around you, you see more of them. You catch one. It's a mayfly, a little more than a quarter inch long, with a grey body and grey wings. It's what we call a baetis, but you don't need to know that. All you need to know is that when you look in your fly box, there's a fly in there that looks pretty close to the same size and color.

In fact, it's called an Adams Special, it's a size 18, and you think the wings show a little bit more white than the insect you caught, but it's close. You try it. You cast your line so the fly lands three feet or so above where the fish has been rising, and lo and behold, the trout rises for your fly, but you're too antsy, and you pull it away too fast. You hope you haven't spooked him. On the second cast, the current takes the fly a little to the left of the fish, and anyway, he's busy eating a real insect. On the third cast, your timing is perfect. He's been rising every few moments, and right as your fly comes overhead, he takes it. You set the hook, and you have a fish on! That's how it works.

Of course, there are countless scenarios on why one fly works better than another. At times, there may be three or four distinctly different insects hatching at the same time, and the fish may be keying on one particular type of insect. Trout are individuals, and it's common to encounter scenarios such as the German brown rising under the river birch eating ants falling off the branches, while the rainbow 20 feet away in the riffle is eating only pale morning dun mayflies. Most times, however, you'll find the majority of the fish eating the same insect during a hatch, and if you can match that insect, you'll catch fish.

Presentation

Once you've figured out which fly to try, the presentation is very important. When a hatch is occurring and the fish are looking to the surface to feed, they are also wary. Most of the danger in a trout's life comes from above, such as herons, eagles, raccoons, and other natural predators. When you disturb the surface by flailing your fly line on the water, you're going to "put the fish down," as we flyfishermen call it. The presentation of the fly to the trout must be as delicate and unobtrusive as possible. When using the casting techniques learned in Chapter Two, it's important to remember that the goal is to catch fish, not just to look pretty while casting the line. A good cast is one that puts the fly into position for a trout to take it, while not spooking the trout.

When presenting a dry fly to a rising trout, it's important to remember that you don't want to bonk the fish on the head with the fly. You want to cast so that the fly lands upstream of the fish and drifts naturally to the fish. The best cast for a beginner to start with is one that is angled 3/4 of the way across the direction of the current—that is, not directly upstream (1) and not directly across the stream (1/2). The fly should drift right with the current—no faster and no slower.

Drift

Every river has currents, no matter how subtle or obvious. When there is an obstruction in the river, like a boulder or a fallen log, the current will be slower downstream of that obstruction. (See Chapter Ten, Reading Water and Approaching Fish). By the same token, the current will be faster where the water encounters less resistance. It's almost like fast lanes and slow lanes on a freeway. Here traffic may be all jammed up, and there the cars are zooming by. When you cast across a river, you may encounter three or four different currents in a 40-foot cast. Take the time to read the water and analyze how you're best going to drift your fly.

Direction of Flow
↓

The Dry Fly Cast (3/4 Upstream)

If the fly is pulled faster than the current or across the current for some reason, it won't look natural to the fish, and they won't strike. That is what we call drag—when the fly is pulled through the current faster than is natural because the fly line itself is caught on the current. If the line simply lays on the water, the current will catch it and pull it in a "U" downstream. The fly then is sped through the water much faster than is natural, which turns the fish off. So it's important to learn to mend.

Mending

Mending is when you flip the line upstream or downstream so it won't drag and disturb the drift of your fly. Mending is a simple technique that is sometimes hard to do well, because it requires some finesse. Mending is accomplished by simply rolling the wrist so that the rod tip lifts the fly line off the water and places the line upstream, eliminating drag. When you've thrown a good mend, the fly drifts along with the current, neither skipping across the current nor floating faster than the current. At some point, the mend will lose its effectiveness, and you may have to mend again.

Though mending is difficult to master, it is one aspect of flyfishing that really separates the men from the boys and the women from the girls. Matching the speed of the current with your drift is essential, and mending is what makes it possible. There are a lot of factors for the beginning flyfisherman to keep in mind, and it can sometimes be overwhelming. Mending sometimes seems like just another distraction to the beginner, but it can really make a difference in catching fish.

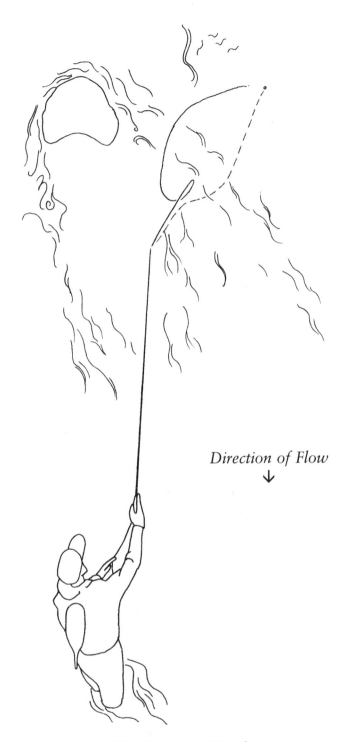

Direction of Flow
↓

The Upstream Mend

44

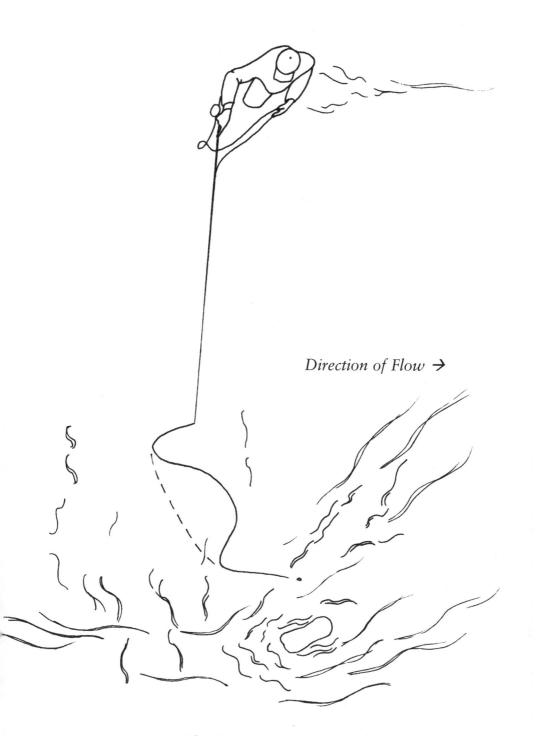

Direction of Flow →

The Downstream Mend

The Reach Cast

One of the most effective ways to mend is to include the mend in the cast before the line even hits the water. We call this ready-made mend a "reach cast." Technically, in a 3/4 upstream cast, it's accomplished by making a normal cast, but once the rod tip has stopped at the end of the cast, you push through with the arm, forcing the line to land either upstream or downstream of where it normally would land. This requires a "reaching" motion, therefore the name. If a normal cast were used, the fly would begin to drag before it reaches its target. This is important because many strikes occur in the first few moments of a drift. Using a reach cast decreases your dependence on mending during the drift.

Ideally, your best drift is the simplest drift, with no conflicting cross-currents. Accordingly, as we mentioned in the previous chapter, positioning is just as important as casting and mending. If you find you must mend to get a good drift, ask yourself this question: if I move to a different spot, can I make a better cast from that position without having to mend? Most of the time, the answer is yes. We realize that sometimes you're

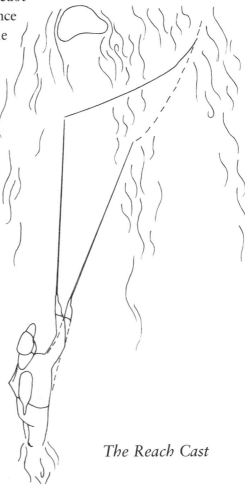

The Reach Cast

Retrieving slack

just not able to find a good position to cast to a rising trout. Maybe the stream is too deep to wade, the current too strong, or there's a logjam in the way. That's when you make longer casts and try mending to get a good drift.

Retrieval

Most of the time you'll be casting upstream. Every now and then you'll encounter a situation that calls for a downstream cast, generally on still, clear spring creeks, but most of the time an upstream cast is preferred. Since you're casting upstream, that means the current will be bringing your line back to you, creating slack in the line the closer it gets to you. You must retrieve that slack, because if a fish strikes your fly when you have 10 feet of slack on the water, there's no way you'll be able to pick up that slack and set the hook before the fish spits out the fly. This is extremely important. In fact, we consider it a dividing line: good fishermen retrieve their slack, and poor fishermen, or let's say those who are still learning, don't retrieve their slack.

Some of the old flyfishing books show a motion where you roll the line between your fingers and your thumb to retrieve the slack, but that's far too slow for all but the most gentle rivers. We recommend stripping the line through the rod hand and pooling the slack at your feet. Stick out a finger on the hand holding the rod. Some people use their index finger, but others prefer the middle finger. Loop the line on that finger, and using the hand holding the line, pull in segments of line a foot or more at a time, using the extended finger on the rod hand to control it. It's like riding a bike. Once you get the hang of it, you'll never forget it. Retrieving your slack is equally important whether you're nymph fishing or dry fly fishing; the axiom is that you shouldn't have slack on the water, because you want to be in a good position to set the hook when you get a strike.

The Strike

Ideally, there should be no more than a foot or two of slack on the water when that strike occurs. Mentally, you should be ready to set the hook NOW, not after analyzing the situation for a second or two. Physically, it's hard to overcome the temptation to set the hook very hard, because your adrenaline will be flowing and you don't know how much strength it takes to set the hook. It actually takes very little strength to set the hook, but it does require speed. Strength is in your shoulder, but your shoulder is slow. Your wrist is comparatively weaker, but the wrist is fast. Use your wrist to set the hook.

Many beginners set the hook either much too hard or much too slow. If you set the hook too hard, the consequences are very negative. First, you'll likely damage the fish, sometimes by literally ripping his lip off. Second, it's very likely that you'll snap off your fly. And third, you don't realize the pleasure of playing a trout on a fly rod. Think about it. The tissue on a trout's mouth is similar to the pad of your thumb. How hard do you have to set the hook to sink it in your thumb? Not very hard.

As you get more experienced as a fisherman, you'll realize that not every strike is the same. It very much depends on what the fish are eating and what type of water you are fishing. Fish are calorie counters. They won't expend more energy rising to a fly than they gain by eating it. For example, when trout are rising to big active hatching insects in fast water, like green drakes or caddis, they typically strike hard and fast, because they know that those bugs may fly away any moment, and a green drake is a pretty good meal. But when the target is an ant struggling in calm water, or a mayfly spinner that has fallen to the water and died, then they know the bugs aren't going anywhere and they take them in a more leisurely fashion. You may set the hook too slow when fishing a green drake and too fast on a spinner fall. Observe how the fish are rising, analyze whether or not you're hooking fish, and adjust accordingly. Our friend Paul Jacobson recommends that you "answer the phone," in other words, simply lift the butt of the rod up to your ear when the trout strikes, and you'll be fast enough to set the hook.

Emergers

Another exciting aspect of dry fly fishing is fishing emergers. The term "emerger" describes the transitional phase when a pupa is hatching. As the insects hatch from the husk of the pupae, they typically surround themselves with a layer of gas bubbles, which helps them float to the surface. When they reach the surface, they often dry their wings for a few moments and fly away. Sometimes you may find it confusing when you're standing on a beautiful stretch of trout stream, insects are hatching everywhere, and you see only an occasional rise. Instead of thinking "there aren't any fish in here," think deeper. Why should the fish rise to the surface to take an insect when they can eat them before they get that far? For a fish, it's easier to feed subsurface than it is to rise to the surface. Often during a very prolific hatch, most of the feeding occurs below the surface. Fly tyers are, above all, observers, and they've certainly noticed this phenomenon. There are emerger patterns for almost every dry fly pattern. They even go so far as to imitate the layer of gas bubbles with a halo of air-trapping filament wrapped around the fly.

Emergers are not, of course, designed to float high on the surface of the water, and it's up to you to determine how deep to fish your emerger. Sometimes trout will take emergers just under the film of the surface, so it's not necessary to weight your fly, or sometimes they'll take them near the bottom, which makes it necessary to weight your leader. A little experimentation should show you how much weight to use. (We'll discuss fishing with weight at length in Chapter Four.) At this point, fishing an emerger with weight is a combination of nymphing and dry fly fishing.

Droppers

It serves to illustrate the point that there are often crossovers, instances where combining different aspects of flyfishing can be very effective. For example, a deadly tandem combination can be teaming a dry fly with an emerger as a dropper. In this scenario, we like to tie a dry fly, such as a caddis, as a lead fly eight or ten feet down the leader. Then we take two or three feet of tippet and tie it directly to the lead fly (either right into the eye of the dry fly's hook, or at the bend in the hook) and hang a dropper off the lead fly. That way, no matter what's working, dry fly or emerger, you've got it covered. Sometimes we even do that with a nymph. We'll tie on a fly like an Elk Hair Caddis and drop a Prince Nymph underneath it, and the dry fly acts as a strike indicator for the nymph. It's surprising to see that you'll often catch fish on both flies over the course of the day. This technique is often very effective when you're casting from a dory floating down the river, when you have only a few seconds to drift through a riffle. Sometimes a hungry trout will take your dry fly on the surface, and other times they'll slurp in the nymph drifting underwater.

Pocket Water

Though dry fly fishing is extremely effective when a hatch is occurring, sometimes dry fly fishing is deadly slow when there is no insect activity. When this is the case, we seek out a place where the fish have no choice but to eat a dry fly. That place is what we call pocket water, where a fast current rushes over boulders and other obstructions, leaving small "pockets" of calmer water that provide a resting place for trout. These trout are hardy, quick individuals who make their living by making instantaneous decisions. They don't have a lot of time to deliberate about whether or not they want to eat an insect; by the time they make up their minds, it's too late. The fly has already swirled past.

Instead, trout in pocket water make quick, aggressive strikes. And because of the turbulent conditions, fishing a small, precise imitation of a hatching insect is usually unnecessary. We prefer to fish bright, bold attractor patterns in pocket water—flies like the H&L Variant, Royal Wulff, Stimulator, and Humpy are some of our favorites. These are flies that really don't imitate any insect specifically, but imitate lots of insects generally. More importantly, their bright colors trigger the trout's impulse to strike, and wham-o, you've got a fish on. Even if there's not a hatch in progress, pocket water trout will still look to the surface for insects, and they'll strike readily.

Scheduling

If you're having a slow day on the river, maybe you should vary your schedule. Our hands-down favorite time to fish is in the evenings. We've never understood why many fishermen's schedules are like an office workday, from 9 to 5. That's often the slowest time of the day. Insects have evolved so that many of the hatches occur right at dusk, when the struggling newborn insects are less visible to fish and birds. That's the time to be on the river, when the trout are slapping the water, the birds are diving for newborn insects, and when you break off a fly on a huge trout, you have to turn to the evening sky and illuminate the eye of the hook against the sunset to tie a new one on. That's when we tell our wives not to expect us until well after dark, and we mean it. We come home at "dark-thirty" with big smiles on our faces and lots of stories to tell.

Gratitude

by John Dietsch

"We are always starting over. We are always beginning again. Something within us or about us changes: it is time to be moving on. Change is seldom easy. A friendship, a favorite spot, a familiar lifestyle slip away, and nothing is the same. The important thing is to be able to sacrifice at any moment what we are for what we could become. May God grace our turning points with patience and peace."

—Miriam Therese

Christmas time has always been the time of year for me to reflect on what I have, and to come to realize that we can take nothing for granted. On the afternoon of Christmas Day I went fishing, and the next day, while skiing, I had a stroke and came as close to death as I ever have.

I had never tried fishing at Christmas time. In years past I'd been too into skiing and snowboarding to even give it a second thought. But last Christmas Day I decided to give myself a special present. I spent the morning with my parents, my sister's family, and my wife opening presents—I got a dress shirt, a tie, a sweater, a couple pair of socks, underwear, etc...not that I didn't appreciate those gifts, but I just decided that I would give myself a present that afternoon. So I bundled up and took myself flyfishing for Christmas.

My parents live on the Roaring Fork River, and upstream from their house there are only about three homes before the road ends and the river enters a three-mile section of catch-and-release-only water accessed by a small footpath. Ice and snow choked the river in the Canyon Section. It was a gorgeous cold winter day, around 24 degrees in the shade, but downright warm in the sun.

I found a section that was moving slowly—a place that I knew was deep and typically held many fish nearby during the summer months. I took off my gloves for a moment, opened my fly box and selected two distinct tiny patterns that caught my eye in their respective places among the others—#20 midge larvae. Just as my fingers began to numb, I finished the clinch knots, and slipped my cold hands back into my gloves. After my fingers warmed up some, I pinched on a weight four inches above the first fly and an indicator about six feet beyond that. To catch trout in the middle of winter in the Rocky Mountains you typically have to use midges, the staple diet of a trout in the coldest months of the year. In this case, I decided to fish them deep since there were no bugs flying and no fish rising.

For the first half-hour or so I thought that perhaps my gift to myself was a bit foolish; ice caked around my line, forming a solid heavy film that made the line feel like a string of lead as I cast. I had to clear the ice off every throw; if I waited too long to clear it, the ice would get so thick that it could not pass through the eye at the tip of the rod. I had to take my gloves off and use the heat of my fingers to melt off the frosty coating. Standing alone on the ice shelf, convincing myself that it would bear my weight as I shuffled toward the slow-moving pool that bore its way through ice flows on the river, I went through the arduous process of casting and clearing repeatedly until I developed an efficient routine.

After hooking and losing a small trout, I shuffled back off the shelf, walked up the path and found a slower, deeper pool upstream. On the third cast I hooked a nice rainbow that gave a surprising amount of fight. Since trout go into semi-hibernation in the winter months, they typically don't fight much. But this one did, and it made me smile. I heard myself say, "nice fish," to no one in particular.

After catching three or four beautiful and darkly mottled rainbows I began walking down the snow-laden path toward home and peered down onto a small eddy formed by the white ice floes.

To my surprise, a well-proportioned rainbow held there in the current and stood out against the pale background as obvious as a beacon in the night sky.

It moved slowly, sipping midges on the surface. Hastily, I bit off my line at the weight, tore off the indicator, and tied on a piece of tippet and a dry fly. In order to avoid approaching the fish from in front of its line of sight I took pains to find a section of cliff where I could "ski" down the slope in my wading boots. Successfully navigating the section, I snuck up from behind the fish—crawling on my gloves and knees. The eddy current was tricky and I made several drifts to no avail.

Finally, on the sixth cast, I watched the fish swim slowly over to my fly and suck it in. I lifted the rod tip and hooked the fish. Like its brethren, it put up a surprising fight, but just before landing it, the leader strafed over a ragged piece of ice and snapped the fish off. I shrugged my shoulders, reeled up the line, and headed home to get warm. The very fact that I had sight-fished to a nice rainbow on Christmas Day and hooked him up on a dry fly was a wonderful gift. However, the real gift—that I had overlooked—was the fact that I could even be there fishing in the first place.

The next day my wife Mollie and I went skiing at Snowmass, which seemed more sane than fishing, especially since a cold front sent the temperatures plunging to the zero mark. We were skiing down our last run when a very strange feeling came over me. Luckily we were stopped midway up the mountain when the left side of my face began to tremble uncontrollably, my eyesight blurred, and I felt like I was going to pass out. I yelled out, "Mollie, something is happening to me!" It was one of the most frightening experiences of my life. After about fifteen seconds, I snapped out of it. Mollie said she thought I'd had a seizure. When I explained the situation to nearby ski patrolmen, they took the situation far more seriously than I expected.

As it turned out, I had a more pronounced partial seizure in the sled on the way down, and another two-minute episode in the clinic. However, no one knew why I was suddenly having seizures—least of all me—who by now was knocked out with Valium.

Within minutes, I was rushed to Aspen Valley Hospital in an ambulance, Mollie by my side. My parents met us at the hospital where a cat scan and MRI revealed a mass in the upper part of my left brain that had bled. "It is highly unlikely that this is cancer, or even a benign tumor," the doctor informed us to our relief. "We think it is probably what we call a cavernous hemangioma." After many more tests and scans there—and at UCLA when I returned home—the condition was confirmed.

The doctors told us that I probably had this "vascular malformation" in my brain since childhood. This type of condition never shows any signs of being there until it "reveals" itself through a seizure or severe headache when you're in your twenties or thirties, and although it is well documented, it is relatively uncommon. And the best news was—it was curable. (Editor's note: it was during such an episode that Olympic gold medalist and track star Florence Griffith Joyner died in her sleep of a ruptured cavernous hemangioma.)

After an angiogram, and similar opinions from three top vascular brain surgeons, I underwent a four-and-a-half hour surgery on January 13th at UCLA. There was never any real risk of being left with "neurological deficiencies" and the doctors had given me a 98% chance of success before the operation, but that did little to alleviate the nagging thought that I might never wake up from the surgery. So when I came to in the recovery room, vomiting liquid, I was relieved to hear them say that the surgery went even better than expected.

I only spent a day in intensive care, and another three days in the hospital. I stayed home from work to recover for another month, and although there have been no lasting effects from the surgery I was, at first, like an invalid. I could barely walk around the outside of my house the first day—and only with the assistance of my wife.

After the first week, I graduated to walking around the block, then slowly worked my way up to a mile, then two miles...I slowly regained my health, and what could have been a cancerous brain tumor or a paralyzing stroke turned out to be a wake-up call that has caused me to appreciate my life now more than ever.

In April, I returned to my parents' house by the river that I love so much. The Fork looked a lot different now with the snow and ice of December long since melted, and there were a few more fishermen. I quietly found a place upstream and around the corner from the nearest angler, where I could be alone...I began casting for the first time since December.

It was a gorgeous spring day, around 60 degrees in the shade, but downright hot in the sun. I found a section that was moving slowly—a place that I knew was deep and typically held many fish nearby during the summer months. Instead of midges, I tied on two distinctive nymphs, a Prince and a Hare's Ear, each that caught my eye in their respective places in my fly box. It was nice to be in that routine again. Tying the clinch knots came more easily than I expected. A tear of joy fell from my face and smoothed the last knot before I pulled it tight. Suddenly, I realized that God had released me back to the waters where I belonged.

Chapter Four
Nymph Fishing

*N*ymphing, as we explained in Chapter One, is fishing with a weighted fly, drifted underwater to imitate the immature insects growing on the riverbottom.

First, however, you have to come to the decision to fish with a nymph rather than a dry fly. Imagine you're standing in a river, looking upstream. There is a nice riffle about three feet deep in front of you, and you think there are fish in there. There is no activity on the surface; no fish are jumping, and there are only a few insects fluttering around on the bushes at streamside. You want to catch a fish. So what do you do next? It doesn't make much sense to fish with a dry fly in this scenario. You decide to try a nymph.

It sounds pretty simple, and it is. Yet for some people, nymph fishing is an intimidating and mystifying thing. If the fishing is decent at all, we can take a couple of complete neophytes, teach them the basics of nymphing, and have them hooking fish within an hour or two. It is an amazingly productive way to fish, and we try to make it simpler than dry-fly casting. But there are three things that a fisherman has to learn about nymphing: the cast, the drift, and the strike.

Rigging

Before you start to cast, however, you need to rig your line for nymphing. So you reach into the stream and pull out a rock. Analyze the insects you find there. Do any look familiar? Then, look in your fly box and pick out a fly that imitates one of the insects that you found on the rock. Now you're ready to rig up. If the river is deep and wide, you might want to try a long leader, say 12 feet. Or, if it's very clear and still, that's another scenario where a long leader is advantageous. On our home river, the Roaring Fork, a 9-foot leader is about right. We usually use a 4x or 5x leader. That's plenty thin. Even if it's a brand-new leader, we trim off the last 18 inches and then tie it on again. (Use a surgeon's knot or blood knot—see Chapter Thirteen.) Why? To give us a place to hang the weight. That knot—anywhere from three to 16 inches above the fly— ensures that the weight, whether the Twist-on or split-shot variety, doesn't slip down the leader to the fly. (Everyone has his own technique of rigging up. It's interesting to note that John uses a split shot three inches from the fly, while Gary prefers to wrap a Twist-on lead weight around the knot 16 inches from the fly, but we both catch fish.)

Then we attach either a single strike indicator or multiple strike indicators to the leader about 18 to 24 inches from the end of the fly line. Some people like to be minimalists, using only a single small indicator, while others make their line look like a string of Mardi Gras beads. It's a matter of personal preference, depending a lot on how good your eyes are. We suggest two medium-sized indicators. Then tie on the fly you've selected (use a clinch knot, see Chapter Thirteen), and you're ready to fish. Or, if you're in the gambling mood, tie on two flies. Simply take another piece of tippet about 18 inches long and, using a clinch knot, tie one end of it right into the eye of the fly. Then tie another fly onto the trailing end of the tippet (clinch knot again), and you're rigged for two flies. We suggest mixing up the two flies with varying sizes, shapes and colors, and that way you'll find out what the fish like twice as fast.

Now let's talk about weight. It takes a little experience to find out what works. You want to put enough weight on the line to sink the fly, but not so much weight that you're always getting snagged on the bottom. Start with one Twist-on or two small split shot. If you get the feeling that you're not getting deep enough or you're not catching fish, add more weight. If you're dragging bottom or not catching fish, take some weight off.

Casting

Okay. It's time to learn the cast. Above all, it must be clearly understood that when using our nymphing technique, there is now weight on the line, either in the form of a small split shot or twist-on weights. That will dramatically change the performance of the line and rod. *The best nymphing cast is thrown directly overhand.* Many people have trouble with this concept. Maybe they didn't play baseball when they were kids, but "overhand" means exactly that—over the top. "Sidearm" means the arm is throwing with the arm straight out to the side. When nymphing, *any form of sidearm cast is bad, because the weight on the line* makes the cast behave differently. If you throw straight overhand and point the rod tip exactly where you want it to go, the fly will go there. But if you throw sidearm, when you stop the rod tip, the fly will keep going past that point. The centrifugal force of the added weight on the line will make your cast go past your target—likely landing your fly in the bushes. Just remember this: *when nymphing, always cast straight overhand* until you learn to control your line like an expert.

There are actually many ways to cast and drift a nymph. However, the technique that is perhaps the most universal and the one that produces the best results for us is the "high-stick" technique using what we call the "water-to-water" cast and a floating line with small weights. Some people use sinking lines to get their fly down deep, but we find them to be cumbersome. The "water-to-water" cast and the "high-stick" nymphing technique is possibly the most productive way to flyfish!

There's an easy way to cast with weight. Just pull 15 or 18 feet of fly line out of the reel, no more, and let the river pull it out straight downstream (make sure the current is flowing fast enough so your fly doesn't catch on the bottom.) Then, lift the rod tip to clear the line from the water a little, and throw the line straight overhand, as we discussed. Plunk. Throw it *from* the water *to* the water. That's what we call the "water-to-water" cast. *Do not false cast!* Don't worry about the "ten to two" or the candy cane loop or any of that. Just plunk the fly upstream and a little further away from you into the river, which is what we call a 3/4-angle upstream. Then you let the fly drift past you until the stream has pulled the line straight downstream, and there you are ready to cast again. When you try to cast a weighted line, you must remember that *you cannot cast a slack line.* The fly line must have tension on it in order to cast it. If you have 20 feet of line out and 13 feet of the line is puddled at your feet, we promise that you will not be able to cast it. Either feed the line into the current downstream, or pull in a few feet until there is some tension on it.

We must emphasize that short casts are very important in nymph fishing. People are often surprised that they'll hook fish eight or ten feet in front of them when nymphing. The truth is that you can usually get much closer to fish that are feeding near the bottom since they feel safer there. Those 45-foot hero casts are completely unnecessary and very counterproductive, unless you're on a very large river. Once you spend half an hour picking the knots out of your leader, you'll see what we mean. *Do not fish with more line than you can control.*

Also, many people want to cast out a long way in front of them. That's usually ineffective with nymphing on fast Western trout streams. As a good rule of thumb, if you're fishing a run about 30 feet long, position yourself 3/4 of the way down the run, and ten or twelve feet to the side of it. If you poke your rod straight out from your belly, the rod tip should be two feet away from the seam you wish to fish.

Drift

Now let's talk about drift. You know you want to cast upstream, because fish face upstream, looking for their next meal to flow to them. But it's very important that your cast makes your fly look just like one of those real insects that has been dislodged by the current. We call it a "dead drift." In other words, none of those real bugs has a line tied to it, pulling it across the current or faster than the current. So your fly has to look as much like the real ones as possible, which means you want to cast at least 3/4 upstream and, above all, avoid giving the fly what we call "action." Don't pull your line across the current or make it go faster than the speed of the current.

Just imagine that your strike indicator is a little piece of driftwood on the surface, unencumbered by any fly line. That's a dead drift, which is ideal. If you cast at an angle across the current, you will certainly get "drag" in your line, which will make the fly drift faster than a natural insect.

As the fly drifts to you, you'll get more and more slack in your line. As a beginner, that's okay for the first hour or so, but you need to make a move to retrieve that slack. That's because you need to be quicker than a fish. Have you ever seen a fish in an aquarium pick a pebble off the bottom and then spit it back out? That's what a trout is doing in a river. Trout make the decision to eat based on mostly visual stimuli—if it looks like food, eat it. That's why you can fool them with an artificial fly. But when they eat that artificial fly, they feel that the texture is wrong, and they exhale it. Immediately they spit it out. It's nothing personal against you, the fisherman. For all the fish knows, it was just like the dozens of sticks, leaves, pine needles and other flotsam that he keys on visually, eats, and then rejects.

But if you have a bunch of slack in your line, when you see the strike indicator pause as it flows downstream, you can't pull in the slack fast enough to set the hook before the fish spits it out. So, just like when you're dry fly fishing, you need to learn to pull the slack in as the strike indicator drifts towards you. Some of the old flyfishing books teach you to roll the fingers on your free hand take up the slack that way. Again, that's far too slow. The current brings the line towards you faster than you can pull it in three inches at a time. So, with the hand that's holding the rod, stick out a finger (we like the middle finger) and hook the line on it with your free hand. Now pull the slack in as it comes

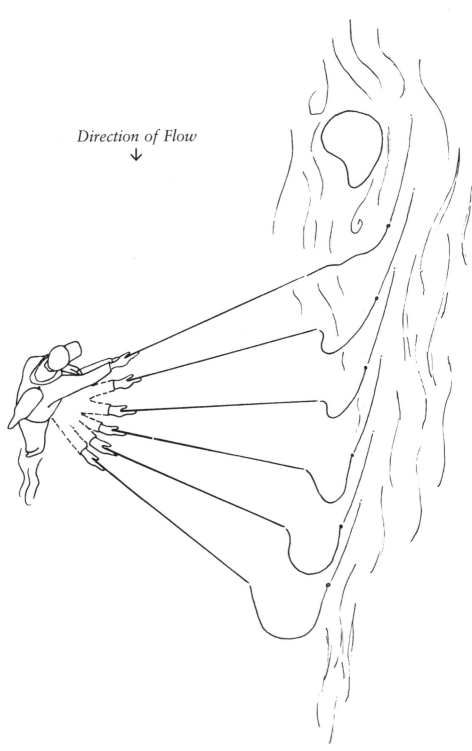

Direction of Flow
↓

Leading—keep the rod tip downstream of the strike indicator

to you with the free hand, controlling it with the finger of your rod hand. That's called the retrieve. With this method, you can bring in the slack 18 inches or so at a time, which means you can keep up with the speed of the current.

It's important to get your act together and start the retrieve as soon as the fly hits the water. Often you'll get a strike within the first few seconds of the drift, and if you still have a bunch of slack out, you'll miss the strike. You can get a jump on starting your retrieve effectively by *always keeping the fly line in your free hand.* Some beginners get lazy and try to fish one-handed, but if you observe expert flyfishermen, you'll rarely see them fishing with one hand. That's because they can control their line and their retrieve much easier when the line is always in hand. Another trick to reduce slack is to simply raise the rod tip.

Leading

Here's another concept that must be introduced: leading. The only way that nymph fishing can be effective is if you keep your line straight and almost taut so that you can see the strike indicator move when the fish strikes the fly. The sequence goes like this: furthest upstream is the fly. Then comes the weight. Then comes the rest of the leader, then the strike indicator. Then comes the fly line, then the rod tip, all in a line. To the greatest extent possible, *the rod tip always leads the drift.* If you get your rod tip upstream of the strike indicator, then the line is making a U, and there's no way to tell if you have a strike.

Combined with keeping the slack taken in, leading makes you an effective nymph fisherman. Really, it's ideal to keep just the strike indicator on the water, and maybe another foot or two of fly line. If you have five or six feet of fly line coiling on the water next to the strike indicator, then you're going to miss strikes, because you can't take up the slack faster than the fish can spit out the hook. On the other hand, you don't want to "tow" your fly through the water, making it drift faster than would be natural, because a fast drift looks unnatural and the fish won't strike.

When nymph fishing, setting the hook takes a special technique, so you'll have to pay close attention when we address that topic in

"Chapter Six: Hooking and Playing a Fish."

Now let's talk about the stages of the drift, and when you can anticipate a strike. There are basically three stages to a nymphing drift: upstream, midpoint, and downstream. The upstream section of the drift is the shallowest, because the fly hits the water and starts to sink. Often you'll get a strike just after the nymph has time to submerge a little bit. As the fly drifts towards you, it sinks ever deeper, and the midpoint of the drift is the deepest. If the fish are laying low on the bottom of the river, the midpoint of the drift is a good place to look for a strike. Remember that a natural nymph is anxious to get back down to the bottom of the river, so a sinking fly imitates this natural action, and the fish respond to it.

But let's not forget the downstream drift. Many fishermen often ignore this part of the drift, because as they move upstream, they tend to think "Been there, done that" and assume that fish that have already seen their presentation won't strike again. Wrong. It's not necessarily the fly, it's the action. After the midpoint of the drift, which is right in front of the fisherman, the fly starts to slowly rise to the surface. Remember our talk in Chapter One about the big picture—hatching insects rise from the bottom of the river to the surface? Well, here's where it comes into play. If the fish are used to seeing insects rising from the bottom to the surface, they'll strike on the downstream section of the drift. In some places, fish are so spooky that you're better off casting downstream to them so

Stages of the drift—upstream, midpoint and downstream

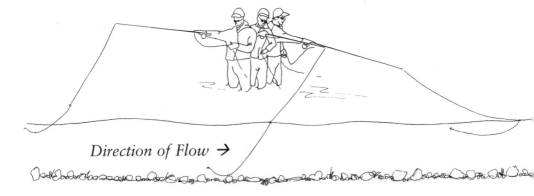

Direction of Flow →

the fly line doesn't drift over their heads, but this is an advanced technique.

Our guiding partner, Paul Jacobson, perfected a method of fishing the downstream drift, which we now call the Jacobson Downdrift. It's a little complicated for a beginning fisherman, but in brief, it involves feeding the slack into the river as the fly emerges downstream, thus imitating the natural action of a hatching or rising insect. It's trickier to set the hook on a downstream drift, because, of course, you can't set the hook downstream. So you have to settle for a quick set to the side, and you'll lose more strikes than with an upstream drift. But, still, you'll catch some, and the downstream drift can be a lot of fun. An added advantage is that the line is all paid out on the current by the time the drift is finished, and that makes it easy to cast again.

Rod Position

If we incorporate rod position into our lesson, then you'll have the finishing touch on becoming a good nymph fisherman. Basically, most people are lazy, in that it's a lot more work to hold your arm above your shoulder all day. Most nymph fishermen prefer to keep their hands near their bellies, with the rod poking into the sky at a 45-degree angle. You can catch fish that way, but you'll lose a lot of fish. Both of us very emphatically believe that it's much more effective to hold the butt of the rod head-high or higher at the beginning of a nymphing drift. Some people call this the "High Stick" nymphing technique. The rod itself is parallel to the surface of the river—pointing straight out, not up. When you have good control of the slack, that puts you in an excellent position to detect strikes. There's a direct line from your rod tip to the strike indicator, and when it even twitches, you can set the hook directly.

As the drift goes by, it's necessary to lower the rod to keep in position to set the hook, but it's a gradual descent. By the time the fly is a midpoint, you should start to lower the rod, and by the end of the drift the rod should be near waist level. (See diagram illustrating depth of drift above)

This holds true regardless of which side of the stream you're on; if you're right-handed, standing on the left bank of the stream looking upstream, you'll have a nice direct cast out into the water.

The Reverse Cast

But if you're left-handed, or if you're on the other side of the river, you'll have to throw the reverse cast, or what Gary calls the Western roll cast. This is simply a back-handed nymphing cast. Everything works the same as the regular nymphing cast, especially the principles of throwing the cast straight overhand and pointing the rod tip directly where you want the cast to go. We find it very helpful to lead the cast by pointing the elbow right at the spot where you want the cast to go, then, starting with the palm of the rod hand pointing down, roll the wrist directly overhand so that the cast ends up with the palm pointing to the sky.

When retrieving a reverse nymphing cast, or Western roll cast, we find that you have an even better opportunity to sense your strikes. If you hold the rod high and straight out, you'll find that you have a "window" to look through—that is, you can look right under your arm to the strike indicator. If you keep the line short and tight, it's possible to really see the strikes well. Again, when you see a strike, you set the hook downstream with a flick of the wrist. On the downstream segment of the drift, the Jacobson downdrift works particularly well. If you throw a little loop in the line just forward of the strike indicator, and feed the slack into the loop as the current pulls it downstream, you'll find a special opportunity to hook fish attracted to the rising fly (this is also called a "stack mend").

As a last note, let us once more emphasize the importance of keeping your line tight. If you have more than a foot or two of slack on the water while nymphing, you will lose strikes. Sometimes we fish a line so short that the strike indicators are all the way out of the water, and believe it, when we get a strike, we know it. Remember, *tight lines!*

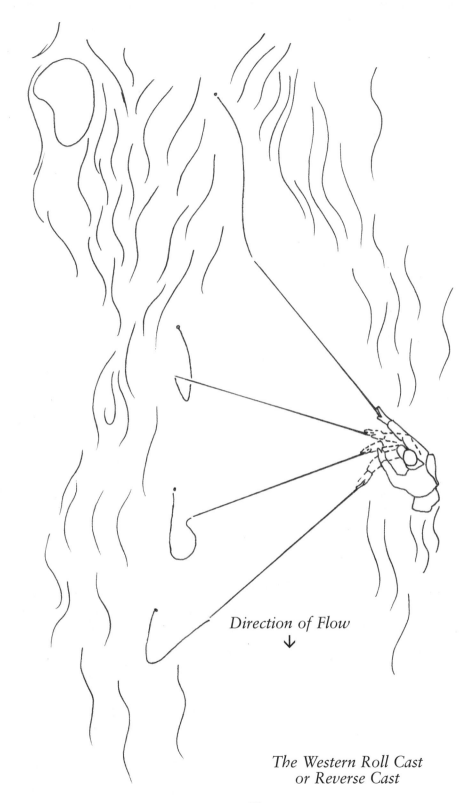

Direction of Flow
↓

*The Western Roll Cast
or Reverse Cast*

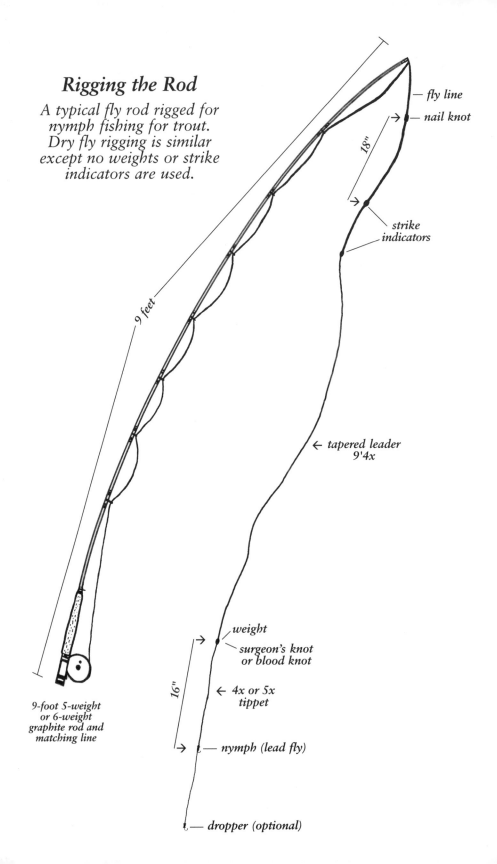

Rigging the Rod

A typical fly rod rigged for nymph fishing for trout. Dry fly rigging is similar except no weights or strike indicators are used.

fly line

nail knot

18"

strike indicators

9 feet

← tapered leader 9'4x

9-foot 5-weight or 6-weight graphite rod and matching line

weight

surgeon's knot or blood knot

16"

← 4x or 5x tippet

— nymph (lead fly)

— dropper (optional)

Firsts

by John Dietsch

In fishing, as in life, there are firsts for everything. The first time I ever caught a trout was on a salmon egg in Cottonwood Creek in the Southern Sierras. I was about six years old. My dad had rigged the pole and told me to go find a pool. I crawled on my belly along a large boulder—I can still remember the smell of campfire in the air, and the way the mist clung to the craggy mountaintops that surrounded me like turrets of a castle. I peered into the mystical swirling waters below me and dunked the egg into the stream. Moments later my body plugged into 1,000 volts of electricity; the tug of that line unknowingly changed my life forever.

I don't know why it is that I love fishing so much, and I have put much thought into it as I am asked that question frequently. Part of it, undoubtedly, is the fact that no one piece of water is ever the same, even five minutes after you've fished it. Going back to your favorite spot always holds something new, as though you were visiting it for the first time.

The first time I ever held a fly rod in my hand was in Vermont at the Orvis Flyfishing School in the early Seventies. My dad took me there the summer after my younger brother died. It provided a wonderful setting for my father and I to bond, and to this day flyfishing with my father provides a certain spiritual renewal for me as it marks the passage of time. Someday, when he is gone, I know that I will look back on those days on the river with him and that will be how I remember him best.

I don't know how Orvis schools teach their classes today, but back then they wouldn't allow you to tie on a fly for the first two days of the school, and it wasn't until the last day that we were allowed to actually fish on the stocked pond. I made a friend that long weekend with a boy named Gus (no relation to the protagonist in *"The River Why"*) who was also at the school with his father. On that last day Gus hooked into the granddaddy trout in the pond, a fish the guides called "Bertha." I remember it like it was yesterday because it was the first time that I experienced what John Gierach calls "fish envy."

"Why couldn't I have hooked that fish?" I remember thinking. Eventually one of the guides took Gus' rod from him and horsed the 24-inch fish to shore since Gus was exhausting him. Gus had tail-hooked Bertha, but it was all the same to me, for it was the largest trout I had ever seen, and I wanted to feel one like that at the end of my line. It took me nearly a decade to experience a hook-up like that, and to this day I will never forget hooking into my first two-and-a-half-footer. It was on Tularec Creek in Alaska, and our guide figured it was about fourteen pounds. I never landed it. And to this day, whether it is my wife that lands a nice one, a colleague who hooks up, or simply a massive fish that broke me off, I long for that 1,000 volts of electricity to pass through my fly rod.

In the mid-eighties I began guiding for the first time. It was in Aspen on the Roaring Fork and Frying Pan rivers. As a green guide I was pretty good at getting my clients into fish, and I prided myself in instructing techniques and demonstrating moves that would catch them trout. However, in that first year, there were several occasions that were "first and last," like the time I grabbed a client's rod when he continued to miss rising fish during a prolific caddis hatch.

In my haste and frustration, I quickly backcast and felt the line stop suddenly behind me. I heard my client grunt, and with all the poise of a plastic surgeon I instantly reached up to his forehead and plucked the Elk Hair Caddis imitation from the middle of his forehead. "Didn't even break the skin," I told him with confidence (what else was I supposed to say?). Of course I apologized, but in some strange way, the unexpected event woke him out of a stupor— and he finally caught on and began hooking fish consistently. It would be the first time that a client ever tipped me a hundred-dollar bill (although I contemplated using similar but more deliberate treatment with lackadaisical clients since then, I have refrained!)

Working on *A River Runs Through It* was full of firsts: Teaching Brad Pitt how to fly cast starting the day after he was hired; scouting rivers in the middle of blizzard conditions—with two feet of snow on the ground—in April, for scenes that were to shoot in August; deciding that the Gallatin River could double nicely for the Blackfoot River; devising ways to shoot fishing scenes with actors who'd never fished before; capturing stoneflies in June and refrigerating them so that we could use them for a scene two months later; transporting farm-raised thirty-inch rainbows and holding them in fish pens along the Gallatin until we needed them for filming; swimming class-three rapids to imitate a lunatic flyfisherman who had a death wish...

And then there were the firsts on the TV fishing commercials I worked on: flying to Japan to make a fly-casting demonstration to a group of advertising executives on an asphalt parking lot in downtown Tokyo; reverse-casting to hit a camera lens from forty feet away for Miller Beer; interacting with imaginary (computer generated) jumping trout as the water exploded with pyrotechnics during a Coca-Cola spot; and directing the first video-based CD-ROM on flyfishing...

But with all the firsts I have had in my career as a flyfisherman, none compares with the "ordinary" experience of simply returning to the river. Each time I return to waters, the same excitement returns and I feel as though I were a six-year-old on Cottonwood Creek going fishing for the first time.

There is something about a river that allows us to look at it, at any given moment, as though we are seeing it brand new for the first time—if only we choose to see it that way. For me the river's simple reminder is that life, indeed, is a precious commodity whose mystery needs to be renewed again and again—a message hidden in rhythmic melodies orchestrated by eddies, runs, and riffles. As Norman Maclean wrote so eloquently, "under the rocks are the words," and some of the words speak to us about our own mortality.

Chapter Five

Trout and Their Behavior

*I*t's possible to catch all kinds of fish on a fly rod, from bass and perch to sailfish and salmon, but we are trout fishermen first, and flyfishing is a wonderful way to catch trout. The trout family is like any other family—its members have different personalities and characteristics.

There are four major species of trout that you might catch on a fly rod: the rainbow, the German brown, the cutthroat, and the brook trout. There are myriad subspecies of each, and also similar species, like char (of which the brook trout is actually a member), salmon, and grayling. But for the most part, if you know the four fish listed above, you'll be in good shape.

Trout share some general characteristics. They have keen eyesight that affords them close to 360-degree vision. They are sensitive to noise, vibration, and movement, and will swim very rapidly when disturbed. They like cool, clean water with lots of oxygen. For the most part, their diet is composed of insects, although as we explained previously, they'll feed on things as diverse as freshwater shrimp, crayfish, worms, terrestrial insects, minnows, frogs, and even mice.

Wild trout are more fun to catch and are hardier than stocked trout. Most fisheries managers are beginning to realize that the wild ecosystem simply isn't suited to "put and take" fishing, whereby trout are stocked in rivers and lakes on a frequent basis, simply to be caught and killed by the worm-dunking public. These hatchery fish have been shown to have a detrimental effect on wild trout populations. In fact, in some states lawsuits are pending to stop "put and take" stocking operations.

It's been shown time and time again that fishing improves dramatically with a decreased creel limit and a "hands-off" management policy that allows trout to reproduce in the wild. Actually, now fisheries biologists have gotten themselves in a real bind. Just as they started to realize that stocking fish was detrimental, it was discovered that exactly that stocking policy had infected many Western trout streams with whirling disease, which dramatically reduces the survivability of wild rainbow trout fingerlings. Whirling disease is a parasite that infects young rainbow trout, and to a degree, other trout species. German browns seem to be somewhat immune to it. It causes the cartilage in their spines to fuse, bending the trout grotesquely so it can only swim in one direction–"whirling" to one side or the other.

Many people assume that trout are constantly on the move, like salmon that are moving upstream to spawn. That assumption is false. Although trout can be migratory, they typically spend the duration of their lives in fairly narrow confines. If you fish a hole and break off a big German brown, chances are he'll be there next month and maybe even next year. Trout find a home in a pool or a riffle and pretty much stay put when they are feeding. Over the course of the seasons, they may move as conditions dictate— spring runoff, low water, winter slowdown, summer heat, and prolific insect hatches all cause fish to move—but generally a fish won't move more than a few hundred yards. The exception, of course, is spawning season, and much like a miniature salmon run, trout will move upstream to spawn. Trout need clean, cool water and small-diameter gravel to spawn, so often they're found mating in small creeks that are tributaries of big rivers and lakes, or, if no creeks are nearby, you'll see them spawning on the edges of rivers and lakes.

In the spawning process, the female scoops out a nest in a gravelly stream bottom (called a redd) so that she can deposit her eggs. The eggs hatch in a little over two months, and the tiny little trout, called "fry," spend their youth in backwaters and the fringes of rivers and lakes. Trout fry are extremely vulnerable to predators and natural factors such as spring runoff, channels drying up, heat, and pollution. Of the hundreds of fry that may hatch from one redd, only a few may reach maturity. As such, the redd is a special place that should be respected. It is considered very poor form to fish over spawning trout, and if you notice a spot where the gravel is bright and clean in the streambed, avoid walking there at all costs. You don't want to crush the eggs before they have a chance to hatch.

Often we are asked "How old is this fish?" when someone lands a trout. Of course, growth rates vary widely considering the factors of different species, habitat, and available food sources, but generally a 12-inch trout is somewhere between two and five years old. A 20-incher may be as much as seven or eight years old. Of course, hatcheries may grow trout faster because of the controlled conditions and consistent feed supply, but it takes time to grow a mature trout. Considering the harsh environment in which they live, it's rather miraculous that so many of them make it to maturity.

Rainbows

The movie star in the trout family would have to be the rainbow. It's a brilliant fish in many ways. First, its coloring is gorgeous. The gill plate of the rainbow is a lovely fuchsia color, and the color extends from the face all the way down the middle of its side. The rest of the body is either silvery gray or green, depending on the subspecies and the feed the fish has been getting, merging to green at the top, punctuated by small black dots. The belly is white. Of course, different strains of rainbows will show slightly different markings and colors. A female rainbow, or "hen," has a rather small mouth and sometimes a more chunky, oval profile. The male, or "buck," is typically slimmer, with a longer jaw.

The rainbow is a showy fish. It tends to the dramatic, both in coloring and behavior. When feeding, the rainbow can be very aggressive, even foolish. The rainbow feeds almost entirely on insects. When hooked, the rainbow is a showboat, leaping boldly out of the water and shaking its head from side to side. It is a strong fish, capable of holding a place in heavy current, and it's also a stubborn fish. A wild rainbow trout will not want to come to your net. It's always fun to guess what kind of fish you have on the line before you actually see it, and there are some indicators that you've hooked a rainbow.

First, the rainbow is very quick. After the hook is initially set, the rainbow likes to charge away from the tension of the line at top speed. It's quite a sensation. You see the strike, set the hook, and zzzzzzzzzzzrrrrrrrrr! Suddenly the fish has stripped out 30 feet of line. If he doesn't succeed in shaking the hook, his next move will often be a jump, arcing a parabola into the air. Sometimes a rainbow will jump three or four times in succession. Then if you bring him in, he'll grudgingly give up line until he sees you, whereupon he'll surge away and renew the battle.

Rainbows love cool water, and they spawn in the spring, right before the snowmelt comes crashing down the rivers. That is when they are most active—during the spawning season. But when the river gets warm, you'll wonder if all the rainbows packed their bags and went on vacation. They'll sulk and refuse to feed, and catching rainbows becomes difficult during those hot days in August.

A nice rainbow specimen will range from 14 to 16 inches and weight between a pound and two pounds. Anything over 20 inches is a very large rainbow, and it's rare to hear of a rainbow weighing more than ten or 12 pounds. The rainbow is a favorite of fisheries managers, because it's so easy to raise and survives well in a wide variety of streams, lakes and rivers, as long as it has clean water and a good food source. For that reason, some professionals call it the "Hereford cow" of the fishing industry. In wide ranges of the West, especially in the Rocky Mountains, the rainbow has been stocked into drainages where it isn't native. If you catch a rainbow in Colorado or Montana, for example, you've either caught a stocked fish or a descendant of a stocked fish.

Browns

But there are other fish to catch, so to speak, and the next is the German brown. The "browns," as they are known, reflect some of the temperament of the European continent from which they were imported. The brown is more reserved, studied, even cunning. It is a very predatory fish. The brown's diet is, of course, comprised of insects to a great extent, but woe to the minnow, sculpin, grasshopper, frog, or even mouse that becomes vulnerable to a big brown. Many is the time that we've caught a 15-inch brown with a six-inch minnow in its gullet. The brown's mouth opens wider than a rainbow's, and the teeth are more prominent, which sometimes makes removing a fly quite a trick.

In general, the brown's profile is longer and skinnier than a rainbow's. Sometimes the head looks twice as big as a rainbow's. While the rainbow carries a silvery sheen, the brown is golden, especially on its side and fins. Its sides are dotted with black and orange spots. It carries no stripes.

As we mentioned, the brown is a cunning fish. If you hook a trout that is reluctant to show itself, it's likely a brown. The brown's initial surge after being hooked is very powerful. We won't say that the browns won't jump—sometimes they do, and spectacularly—but generally they don't jump as often as a rainbow when hooked. More likely, you'll be playing a fish with a good deal of tension on the line, and after a few moments you'll notice the fish isn't going anywhere. So you tug, and you tug a little harder, and darned if that brown hasn't tangled your line on a stick or root underwater. By doing so, he gives himself a solid anchor to pull against, and many times he'll snap your line by pulling against an underwater obstacle. That's a smart fish.

It is said that the older and bigger a brown gets, the more nocturnal and predatory the fish becomes. We know fishermen who catch a lot of big browns, and they don't even start fishing until the sun goes down. They use big streamers, grasshoppers, and even mice patterns. Browns can tolerate much warmer water temperatures than rainbows and cutthroats. They're comfortable at water temperatures up to 65 degrees, and will survive 70 degrees or more, while rainbows suffer and die at those temperatures. German browns spawn in the fall, so they become more active and their colors become more intense towards September and October. German browns can grow very large, with several caught over 30 pounds—a monstrous fish. But a 15- or 16-inch brown is considered a nice, mature fish. If you ever catch a brown over 20 inches and, say, four pounds, treasure the memory. That's an exceptional fish.

Cutthroats

The next member of the trout family, the cutthroat, is actually the native fish for much of the Rocky Mountain region. The cutthroat is so named because of the brilliant orange-red "slash" under its jaw, which almost makes the fish look like it is bleeding. The cutthroat took it on the chin during the days of Western expansion, losing much of its range to overfishing, logging, mining pollution and erosion. When you catch a brown, rainbow, or brook trout in Montana, Wyoming, Colorado, Utah, or New Mexico, you've caught a member of a species that was stocked in the Rocky Mountain waters to replace the cutthroats that were largely exterminated during the late 19th and early 20th centuries.

The cutthroat is an everyman's trout. They're sometimes easily fooled by any old fly or lure; they fight well but not brilliantly; they grow large when conditions allow; and they are a beautiful fish. The brilliant orange-red coloring often extends down the sides and stomach of the fish, especially when they're spawning, though the overall sheen of the fish is a golden color. They bear black speckles, typically more intense near the tail, but they don't have a red stripe down the side like a rainbow. Sometimes you'll see a fish with that tell-tale cutthroat slash, but with markings more like a rainbow, with a stripe down the side. That's what we call a "cuttbow," or a hybrid rainbow/cutthroat. The two species are so closely related that they are capable of interbreeding.

Cutthroats like clean, pure water, and they like it cold. We've found them at lakes over 12,000 feet in elevation, where ice is the prevailing condition six or seven months out of the year. Like rainbows, they rely on aquatic foods most of the year. Cutthroats spawn in the spring, which may mean June or July in the high-country terrain. Cutthroats can be fickle, too, as is always the case when you're fishing high-country lakes. Sometimes they'll eat anything you throw at them, and other times not even the most precise imitation of a natural insect will interest them. As with any fish, a cutthroat's size at maturity depends largely on its habitat and food supply. We once saw a crew of fisheries biologists conducting a population survey on a tiny high-alpine stream three feet across, and yes, there were cutties in there, though a mature fish was only five or six inches long. Then again, some of the cutthroats in Yellowstone Park routinely reach 20 inches and five pounds. Typically, a nice specimen will range from 12 to 16 inches, with the rare fish coming in at over 20 inches and six or seven pounds.

The knock on cutthroats is that they don't fight as strongly as a rainbow or a brown, but display a kind of rolling, thrashing motion when they're hooked. Personally, we can think of no greater sport than catching native cutthroats in a clean Rocky Mountain lake or stream. Cutthroats are beautiful trout, and when you're catching them, you're usually in a beautiful locale.

Brookies

The fourth fish you'll encounter as a flyfisherman is the brook trout, which, as we mentioned, is not actually a trout, but a char native to the Atlantic seaboard. If you look on one of those trout species charts that you see in fly shops, you'll see the brook trout lumped together with the Dolly Varden, the lake trout and other char.

Flyfishermen have somewhat of a love-hate relationship with "brookies," as we call them. They're eager little fish, snapping at anything that comes their way, so they're easy to catch. Unfortunately, many of the brookies found in the West are a stunted variety that was planted many decades ago. In a way, brook trout are like pigeons. They're so successful at reproduction and so forgiving to humans that they make a pest out of themselves. More than a few streams in the Rocky Mountains have been all but ruined by the introduction of these brook trout. Instead of a few hardy, healthy cutthroats, you'll find a horde of stunted little brookies. Though we're heartily in favor of practicing catch and release, brookies are a different story. They breed so successfully that they are capable of outstripping the habitat, so that none of them are capable of reaching any size. You'll actually be doing them a favor by thinning them out. Besides, they can be a delicious reminder of why we have the instinct to fish in the first place.

Brook trout spawn in the fall, and much of the reason for their success in reproduction lies in their spawning methods. While the other three trout species require oxygenation of the eggs with a clean, fresh, constantly renewed water supply, that's not necessarily so for the brook trout. The brook trout can lay its eggs in an all-but-stagnant pond and they'll still hatch. That's why you'll find brookies in beaver ponds, swamps and other still waters.

In appearance, brook trout are a pretty fish. Their sides are deep green, marked with light-green squiggles and dotted with orange and black spots, which is why they're sometimes called "speckled trout." The fins and stomach are a yellowish-orange, and the fins carry a white strip on the front. Though it's possible to find very large brook trout that weigh in excess of four pounds and longer than 20 inches, that's very rare. Most full-grown brookies never grow longer than eight or ten inches. A 12-incher is considered a nice fish.

In the waters of their native Newfoundland, Nova Scotia, and the Eastern Seaboard, there are places where brook trout inhabit big water and grow very large. But in the American West, their stunted strain has been planted in little trickles of streams and isolated ponds. We have had a blast catching brookies in water where you can hardly get your ankles wet.

As we mentioned, each of these four species is a general species. Trout are a fascinating fish, in that they can be found almost anywhere in the world that has clean, cool water. (John has caught them in a creek only minutes away from the famous surf town of Malibu, California.) Over the millennia, trout have adapted to extremes of temperature, drought, weather, water flow, and predation. There are literally hundreds of subspecies of trout that are found in all kinds of exotic locations, and some of these fish are endangered. There are desert trout in Arizona and Mexico, golden trout in the high mountains of Wyoming and California, greenback cutthroat trout in the upper Snake River, and landlocked salmon in the Columbia River Basin. Trout can be found in Costa Rica, Argentina, South Africa, New Zealand, Europe, England, Greenland, Russia, Japan, and other places too numerous to mention.

Salmon

It would be a mistake, of course, to close this chapter without mentioning salmon, because catching a salmon on a fly rod can be one of life's most exhilarating accomplishments. Silver, Atlantic, King, humpback—there are all manner of salmon in all manner of places, from Scotland to Norway, Greenland and the Great Lakes, to the great Pacific Northwest, including British Columbia and Alaska, to Chile, Argentina and practically anywhere there are clean rivers feeding into oceans. There are many various species of salmon weighing from less than half a pound to more than a hundred pounds, and sometimes there's no clue what you have on the line until the fish is in the net.

Flyfishing for salmon is a whole different ball of wax. A salmon's sole mission is to reproduce, not eat, so you're wasting your time if you think you're going to match the local hatch and see a salmon eat your fly. He's not interested. You can, however, provoke a salmon to strike a fly out of reflex, irritation, or simple aggression, and that's why salmon flies are typically so gaudy—to get the fish to notice them. And, of course, a salmon is a big fish typically swimming in deep, heavy water, so salmon fishing demands a heavy rod, reel and line. A nine-weight rod is typical for salmon fishing, and that entails a lot of hard work to move that heavy rod and line all day. (Although in recent years, anglers have started using smaller rods and nymphs to catch salmon.)

Lastly, we should mention that flyfishermen are pursuing all kinds of fish in all kinds of locales—tarpon off Florida and Africa, corvina in southern California, sea trout and redfish off the Texas coast, sailfish off Mexico and Costa Rica. If the fish can be fooled with a hook wrapped with feathers and fur, somebody's going after them, simply because it's so much more fun to catch a fish on fly gear.

It Was A Big Brown

by Gary Hubbell

It's interesting to note how fish can exhibit personalities, especially when they're big ones. In fact, you can often tell the species of a trout simply by observing its behavior when it's hooked. John can tell you all about that. It was a beautiful midsummer day in Montana, and we were fishing DePuy's Spring Creek outside Livingston. That is my definition of living right.

It also happened that we were working—John was directing fishing sequences for *"The ESPN Flyfishing School"* CD-Rom, and I was the still photographer on the set. On this particular sequence, John was also the talent, teaching a pretty young lady named Priscilla to nymph fish. (Sounds like fun, doesn't it?) After we got set up and the cameras were rolling, John started to demonstrate for Priscilla. The lesson was progressing nicely, the footage was rolling, and as John was almost ready to hand the rod over to Priscilla, he got a strike.

Really, it was as obvious a strike as you'll ever see. The strike indicator simply stopped dead in its drift. John set the hook, and the war was on. By the bend in his rod, I could tell it was a large fish right from the beginning. I was watching through a long lens, snapping frames as the action progressed. The fish ran upstream until it was stymied by a waterfall, then bolted downstream, stripping line off John's reel like a drag racer. In the first 30 seconds, I was thinking, "This has got to be a big brown."

How did I know? Well, rainbows typically exhibit themselves when they're hooked. By that, I mean they jump, depending on the constraints of the water. Sometimes a rainbow will make three or four or even five big, splashy jumps, shaking its head and slamming back into the water during a fight. They're pretty straightforward. A German brown, on the other hand, is more devious. They'll submarine deep into the water, then wrap the line around a tree root or piece of driftwood protruding into the water. Once they've got something solid to resist against, they'll snap the line.

This big brown performed as if scripted, and indeed, the cameras were still rolling. There was only one log in the stream for 50 yards in each direction, but that's where he went. The trout was so big and strong that John was powerless to stop him. The log was in shallow water next to the bank, and John reeled up slack as he waded to the log. The bend in the rod was not lively anymore—just a steady, dead weight. John approached the log carefully, should the fish have chosen to spook back into the main current, but it wasn't necessary. Ultimately John ended up on his belly, leaning over the log and peering into the dark water for a fish that wasn't there anymore.

When he stood up and kicked at the water in frustration, John yelled "Cut!" but the crew was laughing too hard to shut the cameras off, and his frustration was recorded for our evening viewing pleasure. Though we had fun at John's expense, we all knew that he had done a beautiful job playing the fish—it's just that not very many of those big browns end up in the net, no matter what you do.

Chapter Six:

Hooking and Playing A Fish

Hooking a fish is without question the most exciting part of flyfishing. That singular moment when you know the trout has accepted your fly and you realize you're about to set the hook—well, that's one of the finest things in life. We can preach to you forever about the correct cast, presentation, and drift, but that all goes out the window when it's time to hook the fish. We've guided folks who could do everything right except set the hook on a trout and play him into the net. There really is an art to it.

Dry Fly Hook Set

Let's start with dry fly fishing. First, if there are trout rising around you, observe how the trout are taking the natural insects. There are many kinds of rises, relating to different hatches, currents, even the size of trout, but we're not going to get into that kind of detail in this book. Just remember that trout are calorie counters. They're not going to expend any more energy than necessary to eat a fly. If they're calmly sipping in little tiny midges, the rise will be delicate and unobtrusive. It's going to be a delicate take, and therefore you need to make it a delicate set of the hook. Conversely, if you're fishing the green drake hatch and it sounds like someone is throwing fist-sized rocks in the river every time a fish rises, better be on your toes and set the hook fast and hard, because that's how the fish are rising.

Flyfishing is a visual sport, not tactile. For all you folks that have learned to set the hook by feeling little tugs on your line, forget that concept. When you see the strike, set the hook. You won't feel it. Timing is essential, with quickness paramount. Only occasionally in flyfishing will it be necessary to pause and wait for a fish to take the fly before setting the hook. When you see the take, set the hook, *right now*. When fishing in a current, the trout knows it only has a split second to take the fly drifting over his head, so his strike is usually very quick. Sometimes trout will take in something that isn't food by mistake—like a duck feather or a dandelion seed floating on the water. Once they realize that the texture and feel is wrong—"this isn't food!"—they instinctively spit it out as soon as possible. That is what will happen with your fly if you don't set the hook immediately.

When you set the hook, you must know how much power to use. Really, it's a matter of quickness, not strength. The power in your upper body is in your shoulder, which is what many deep-sea or surf fishermen use to set the hook on heavy ocean fish. But your quickness is in your wrist. Think about it: all you're trying to do is drive a sharp little hook into some tissue that's about as tough as the pad of your thumb. How much strength do you need? When you connect that fly to a line and a nine-foot fly rod, not much. Use your wrist to set the hook. Give it a quick little upwards flick. Remember that trout have delicate mouths. When you give it a hero jerk to set the hook, you can literally rip the lips off the fish, or you can break the line, leaving the hook in its mouth. That's unfair to the trout.

Some people have a great deal of difficulty discerning where their fly is, and whether or not the fish rose to their fly or a natural insect, especially with small flies in low-light situations. We have some suggestions. First, keep an eye on your fly line, and realize that your fly will be eight to 14 feet away from the end of your fly line, depending on your leader length. Look for the profile of your fly, and if a fish rises within two or three feet of where you think your fly is, go ahead and set the hook. You'll be surprised at how many times that fish is indeed rising to your fly. If you're wrong, so what. Cast again. Another trick is to tie a large, visible fly like a Royal Coachman or an H&L Variant to your tippet. Then tie another piece of tippet right into the eye of the attractor fly, and tie the pattern you're really interested in fishing about 16 inches down from the attractor. That bold fly will help you easily locate your smaller, less visible fly, and you'll be happily surprised when you hook fish on the attractor pattern, too.

When fishing a dry fly, one of the only exceptions to the "hook fast" rule is when you're fishing still water. For example, trout in a lake sometimes have a long time to look over a fly, and they rise in a leisurely fashion. If you're too fast, you'll jerk the fly away before the fish can take it. It's hard to counteract a good set of reflexes, but sometimes you have to consciously think "WAIT!" and give it a one-count pause before you set the hook. Our partner Paul calls it the "answer the phone" hook set. When you see the take, set the hook with almost the same upward motion and speed with which you would bring the telephone to your ear. This process is often repeated, in an even slower fashion, when saltwater fishing for species like corvina and bonefish.

Nymphing Hook Set

Nymph fishing is different than dry fly fishing, especially when setting the hook. Because the fly is weighted, drifting underwater, you can't see the fish taking it. The only clue you have is given by your *strike indicator* which is like a small floating bobber attached to the leader, usually seven or eight feet away from the fly. Strike indicators come in various forms: yarn; styrofoam stick-ons; hard plastic beads with toothpick-type stays; and malleable putty, all in various neon colors. The object is to attach the strike indicator so it floats on the surface and tells you what's happening down below the surface.

As with dry fly fishing, *the strike is visual. You will not feel it.* You must learn to recognize the strike as a hesitation in the drift. The strike indicator is a little orange dot floating down the current. When its drift is interrupted, set the hook. It's that simple. Once again, you must understand that trout key visually on their food. Your hair-and-feather fly looks like food to them, but as soon as they eat it and find out the texture is wrong, ptooey, they spit it out. It's nothing personal. They eat a lot of stuff that isn't food—

we've cleaned trout that had bits of leaves, pine needles, and all sorts of little flotsam in their craws. They're not down there thinking "Boy, I wish that guy from Indianapolis would quit throwing that fly in my face!" It's much simpler than that. They eat your fly, it tastes wrong, they spit it out, and sometimes they get spooked. To catch fish, you have to set the hook faster than the trout's reflex to spit out the fly. We know we've told you this already, but it's very important information—when you get a strike, set the hook at once.

Because there are many obstructions underwater, like rocks, sticks, and weeds, sometimes when you're nymphing it gets confusing as to whether that's a fish or an underwater obstruction that made your drift stop its progress. There's an easy answer to this: *strike at anything.*

Admittedly, nymph fishing is more frustrating than dry fly fishing, because many times you'll set the hook when it is, in fact, a rock or stick that's hanging up your fly. But if you start trying to guess what it is underwater before you set the hook, you'll be too slow. If you set the hook ten times and nine of those ten times it's nothing, that still means you're hooking a fish one time out of ten. Of course, with experience you'll be able to tell better what's what, but for beginners we always advise *"Set the hook!"*

Having Faith

This is very important. Setting the hook is where flyfishing really borders on religion, as Norman Maclean wrote in the opening lines of *"A River Runs Through It:"* You must believe that there's a fish down there that is inhaling your fly. If you don't believe it, you're sunk. Believing is everything. We've both guided dozens of people who refused to believe that there are actually fish in the river who would actually attempt to eat their fly. For these people, the strike indicator is drifting along nicely when it suddenly halts and quickly submerges two or three times, then is set free. Then they look at us and say, "Was that a fish?"

Invariably, our reply is, "Did you set the hook?"

They'll say, somewhat sheepishly, "No, I thought maybe it was a rock."

And we'll reply, "Well, you'll never know if it was a fish unless you set the hook in time. But I would have set the hook on that one, and I think it was a fish."

When setting the hook on a dry fly, it's simply a matter of quickly lifting up your rod tip; but nymph fishing up and across demands a different technique. The great majority of fish that take your nymph will be facing upstream in a river or creek. If you set the hook by pulling the fly upstream, you'll actually be creating slack or pulling the fly out of the fish's mouth. But if you set the hook with a quick flick of the wrist downstream, you'll be setting the hook into the fish's mouth. ***When nymphing upstream, always set the hook downstream.***

For those of you with big-rod backgrounds like surf casting, deep-sea fishing and bass fishing, be advised that it isn't necessary to really haul back on the rod to set the hook. Strength isn't necessary—speed is. All you have to do is drive a little hook into a trout's lip, and that doesn't take a lot of strength. The shoulder is the strongest part of your upper body, and many fellows with deep-sea experience like to use their shoulder and even their hips to try to set the hook on a trout. Not only is that complete overkill (way too much force), it's also dreadfully slow. Trout are much faster than that. We'll say it again. ***Use your wrist to set the hook.*** It's fast, and it's much easier on the mouth of a trout.

Playing the Fish

Once the hook is set, playing the fish is the same whether you're dry-flyfishing or nymphing. First, any of you who have fished with spinning rods for bass or trout must forget what you've learned. With a spinning rod, the rod is stiff enough and the line strong enough that you can usually reel a fish right on in with little debate. That's not the case with a fly rod. The fly rod is so light and whippy and the line so light that when you attempt to "horse" a fish (play it roughly, dragging the fish in when it's still fighting hard), you'll usually find yourself tying on new tippet and a new fly after the fish has snapped your line. It is a delicate balance between the current, strength and weight of the fish and the small hooks, light tippet and whippy rods of flyfishing.

Most beginners' first instinct is to clamp the line tight to the rod with their fingers, and then attempt to haul the fish on in. WRONG. That instinct must be strongly resisted. In fact, because the fish is usually heading for somewhere far away from you, the first reaction must be *give him some line.* Fly tackle is light tackle. Most of the fun of flyfishing is playing the fish into the net, and that involves a give and take. He wants line, you give it to him. He gives up some line, you take it in.

It is extremely important to remember that there's very little keeping the fish on the line. Sometimes the only thing keeping him hooked is the pressure of a tight line. We've landed hundreds of fish where the hook fell right out of the fish's mouth once the line was slackened. *When playing a fish, always keep the line taut.* That is an essential edict of flyfishing. Do not allow the line to go slack when you're playing a fish. The line should be taut from the rod tip to the fly. At the same time, be sure to give the fish line when he demands it by letting the line feed out freely to the fish. Another cardinal rule is to *Keep your rod tip up.* If constant rod pressure is applied to the fish properly, the line will not break because the fish doesn't have anything solid to resist against. He's resisting against something flexible, yet strong (the rod tip). That tires him. If you keep the rod tip nicely bent against the line, you're tiring the fish and making him work. But once you drop the rod tip and point it at the fish, he's suddenly got something very solid to resist against: your chest. *Snap.*

Very often you'll be in the midst of collecting a bunch of slack line and letting it pool around your feet when you set the hook on a fish. It should be your goal to get that slack line collected as soon as possible when playing the fish. Some of it you can let slip out as the fish pulls away, and the remainder you should carefully reel in. Then you can fight the fish from your reel, which has a built-in drag that lets out line according to the amount of resistance the fish places on it. It's a more reliable system that way. Often you'll find yourself adjusting your drag to reflect the particular conditions of current and size and strength of a fish, while in the middle of fighting him.

Although the reel is mechanical, and you think you might have a better feel for things than the reel, the reel never gets caught by surprise. We've seen many, many fishermen playing a stout trout, happily clutching onto the fly line, when suddenly the fish surges and parts company with the line. Sometimes you just can't react as fast as a fish. By the same token, when reeling in a fish, only keep your thumb and forefinger on the reel crank when you're actually reeling. If you hang on to the crank, the fish can gather his energy and surge away while you've forgotten he's still got so much power. It's amazing how strong your grip can be—strong enough so that a good fish can easily snap your line if you carelessly hang on to the reel crank when he's going for a run.

Again, play it by give-and-take. When the fish yields line, reel him in. When he's surging away from you, let him strip line off the drag. However, don't get caught flat-footed. Many beginners think landing a fish is like playing tennis—you don't move off the court. That's not true. In big rivers with heavy current, you might find yourself running down the bank, crawling over piles of driftwood, dodging boulders and stumbling through the water. In fact, just such a personal recollection was the genesis for the scene in "*A River Runs Through It*" where Paul lands the monster trout. (see sidebar)

Use every tool at your command. The fly rod is a flexible tool, so use it. Think tactically: always keep the pressure of the rod perpendicular to the fish, and keep the fish away from structure in the river. For example, if the trout is running hard toward a submerged log on the right bank of the river, bend your rod hard to the left bank. If he's surging deep to a pile of rocks on the bottom of a pool directly in front of you, hold your rod tip high above him. If he's sprinting towards a fast, strong rapid, steer him around to a pocket of calmer water where you can fight him. Make him fight against that strong, flexible rod tip.

Landing the Fish

As you get more experience playing trout, you'll find how much pressure can be put to bear upon them. Aside from the initial surge immediately after the fish has been hooked, most beginners don't put nearly enough pressure on the rod. If the fish is staying put somewhere out in the stream for an extended period of time, chances are you're not playing him strongly enough. Don't let a fish loaf around and gather his strength. The longer he's on the line without moving, the more strength he has, and the greater the chances he'll slip the hook somehow. Lean into the rod a little bit and see how he responds. Chances are he'll get motivated and go on a run, stripping line out from your reel. Then he'll get tired and you can bring him in closer.

Also, remember that it's unfair to the fish to play him for an extended period of time if you plan to release him. A long, extended battle can weary a fish to the point where he can't recover. It takes a certain amount of strength to maintain a position in a current, and if that reserve of strength is gone, the fish will turn sideways or upside down and will be pulled away by the current and he'll die. With time, you'll learn to appreciate that fine line (literally) between playing a fish too hard and not hard enough. A good rule of thumb is to bring the fish to the net once the fish begins to turn on its side. Don't be too ginger about playing a trout. Your rod is a powerful tool, so use it. Enjoy the fight, but get the fish in and get the hook out quickly so you can set him free.

When netting or landing a fish, there are a few important principles to remember. Some folks say always net a trout head-first. Others say always net him tail-first. We say just do it quickly. A good flyfisherman nets a fish like Mike Tyson throws a punch: it doesn't take very long. Position the fish by holding your rod high above your head, then surface him as close to your legs as possible, then stab the net into the water and come up underneath the fish. We've found that if you prolong the fish thrashing about on the surface of the water, you're likely to lose the fish. Keep him submerged until you're ready to use the net.

If you can competently land a fish without using a net, all the better, because netting can be more damaging to a trout than simply slipping the hook from its jaws and letting it swim away. But most beginners do a poor job of landing a trout without a net, so we suggest that you get a good trout-friendly net (one that doesn't strip away their protective coating of slime or abrade their sensitive skin) and learn how to use it. We've written an entire additional chapter on the details of handling and releasing fish, so please read it and learn how to take care of the beautiful trout that you'll be catching and releasing.

Thinking Like a Fish

It's important to spend some time thinking like a trout when you're playing one. That way you can anticipate what the fish will do. For example, our partner Paul Jacobson, ever the innovator, sometimes practices the opposite of the technique of momentarily "horsing" a fish. Once we saw him hook a solid fish in heavy water, and the trout immediately went on a wild run toward some rapids, which would have certainly meant losing the fish. Paul immediately slackened the line dramatically, and the fish stopped its run. Then Paul leaned into the rod and guided the surprised fish into a calmer pool to finish the fight. We marveled at his presence of mind. "Well," he said, "I knew if he got in those rapids, I was going to lose him, so I gave him some slack so he'd think he wasn't hooked anymore. Then he swam back to his spot, and then I had him."

Wow. We thought Paul was growing gills, he was thinking so much like a fish. It's difficult for the beginner to think like that, of course, because a beginner doesn't have those years of experience and observation. But it's most important that you keep your eyes and ears open and learn something while you're on the water. In fact, that's what many flyfishermen enjoy most about the sport— they learn something new every time they go out. When you're playing a trout, expect the unexpected, and you'll still be surprised.

The Flyfishing Stunt Man

by John Dietsch

It was late in the afternoon in Livingston, and as I drove over the pass toward Bozeman, I realized that there was no sense in scouting locations. Dark clouds were hanging over the Gallatin Mountains to the west. I drove on back to the set where Robert Redford and the rest of the crew were shooting the scene of Brad Pitt and the gang sitting on the steps of the courthouse in *"A River Runs Through It."* It began to rain, and several grips ran around trying to cover up the equipment.

A production assistant came up to me and said that Redford wanted to meet with me in his trailer.

I had been waiting for this meeting for six weeks—six weeks of scouting locations on the Blackfoot, Gallatin, and Boulder rivers, teaching the actors to cast, poring over the script to make sure the fishing scenes made sense. Six weeks of preparation, and all my information was accumulated in a big red notebook— which I had left at the office in Livingston!

Panicked, I made a call to have a PA bring over the notebook, which would take at least half an hour. Unprepared and nervous, I walked into the trailer, the kind of trailer you see on the highway on a summer day, the one you can't seem to pass on a winding mountain road. It was nothing fancy, just a john, a kitchen, a table, and a couch.

"Hi, Bob," I said. Everyone called him Bob.

He smiled that incredibly disarming smile of his and said hello. He shifted over and the various writers, producers and costume designers made room for me at the table. The rain struck the roof of the trailer with a melodious pitter-patter as Redford talked about the fishing scenes. He had a definite vision and was able to express ideas with the kind of grace that has made him so famous. Nothing was ever set in stone. Rather, he had a general view of how things should look. The details always seemed to fall into place once the focused vision was laid out. He was a master filmmaker, and I was about to share my ideas with him on the greatest flyfishing story ever told. It was one of the greatest moments of my life, except for the fact that my notes were in a car traveling somewhere over Bozeman Pass.

Ten minutes into the meeting, I still hadn't needed my notes. As we discussed the storyboards, time passed quickly, and before I knew it, there was a knock on the door. The PA had arrived with my notebook just as I needed it. No one seemed to notice just how relieved I was. Redford then went through each fishing sequence, scene by scene, and gave us his vision of how the scenes should be shot. He suddenly skipped to the last sequence and looked up at me and said, "Is there anything we can do with the final fishing scene? The way it's written in the book and the script, it's too much like the other scenes. We need something more exciting..." his voice trailed off.

There was a long pause that seemed to last an eternity. I had to think fast. From a dramatic point of view, the problem with the last scene was the way Norman's brother Paul catches the large fish while fishing from the far bank; once he lands it, he decides to cross the river in a swift section instead of walking down below and crossing where it is safer. On his way he slips and goes under for a moment. For Norman it was a subtle way to foreshadow his brother's impending death. But for Redford it was too subtle and too much like all the other fishing scenes. It needed more of an edge.

Then it came to me.

"What if Paul sees a huge fish just below a rock at the top of a big rapid," I said with enthusiasm. "He tries to get a good drift, but the fish won't take," I continued, gaining confidence. "The fly is dragging because of the swift current between him and the pool where the fish is. He needs to get closer to get a better drift. So he inches out to the edge of the seam on the rapid, barely holding on. His feet are slipping. But from this vantage point, he can keep the rod high enough to keep the leader just above the fast water to get a decent drift. He casts. The fly lands gently." I paused for effect.

"And kerpow! This huge 'bow erupts out of the water, takes the fly and screams downstream in an explosive run." I stood up

Photography by Gary Hubbell

Fish were rising to dry flies during this March snowstorm, Carbondale, Colorado

Cutthroat trout

Fishing pocket water on the
Upper Frying Pan River in Colorado

Drifting the Yellowstone River near Livingston, Montana

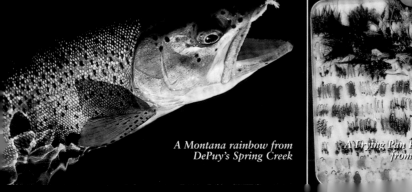

A Montana rainbow from DePuy's Spring Creek

A Frying Pan River fly box from Steve Avery

Montana mayfly

Stonefly nymph

The "H&L Variant"
--early and modern versions

A cutthroat from the Green River

The North Platte River near Saratoga, Wyoming offers some interesting structure

Paul Jacobson with Roaring Fork River rainbow

John Dietsch with Colorado brook trout

Jerry Siem shows his casting skills on DePuy's Spring Creek in Montana

German brown trout

Colorado high-country brook trout

Montana cutthroat trout

Still photographs from the filming of
"A River Runs Through It"
by John Kelly

From left to right - Jason Borger performs the Shadow Cast;
Brad Pitt on the set; John Dietsch and John Bailey instructing Craig Scheffer

From right to left - John Dietsch doubling as Norman Maclean; Dietsch with Redford;
Flyfishing consultant George Croonenberghs and friend with Redford;
Dietsch, grip Johnnie Hale, and Redford on the river.

and leaned back, holding up my arm like I was playing a fish. "Paul tries to play the fish from where he is, but it's huge. It screams downriver, into his backing. He makes a split-second decision to enter the river. He has to swim the rapid while playing the fish."

I stopped. Redford looked me right in the eye.

"And then what?" he asked. I explained that Paul swims the rapid, fights through the waves and negotiates the rocks. At the end of the fight, he stands up in the tail of the pool and hoists the behemoth trout in the air, grinning.

"Do you know where we'd shoot this?" Bob asked, obviously interested.

"Yeah, I think I know the exact spot," I replied.

"So now you're a stunt man." I heard the distinct French accent of Philippe Rousselot, Director of Photography. I turned around. "Look, John," he said, "I have shot stunt men jumping off cliffs in Switzerland and fighting in the rain forests of South America, but I have never killed anyone. I don't intend to start now." After an awkward pause, he asked me if the stunt was safe.

"Yes, I'm sure it's safe," I replied with as much confidence as anyone could muster. I was about to swim a class three rapid without a helmet or life vest.

"Good," he replied. "We're going to do five takes."

My jaw dropped. I had expected to swim the rapid once, maybe twice. Then I remembered. This was show business.

A huge crane angled out into the middle of the river, where it hung just two feet above the roaring Gallatin River. I positioned myself on top of a large boulder at the head of the rapid. Just before jumping into the frigid water, I told Jerry Siem to drop a weighted plastic bottle attached to my fly line into the water ahead of me to simulate the running fish. This had worked just right in rehearsals.

The assistant director yelled "Action!" The cameras rolled. I signaled Jerry to drop the bottle and I jumped into the torrent. The water was freezing, but I had a wetsuit on underneath my clothes. I aimed for the camera as best I could, but the bottle was not in front of me. It was behind me! Suddenly the fly line tightened and spun me around. The rod shot out of my hands and a massive wave smashed into me and I went under. All went quiet.

Under the water and upside down, I waited for the current. I thought about Norman's father, who believed that if you listened hard enough, you could hear the words beneath the river. I listened hard but heard only silence. Then the words came. They were my own: "Jesus Christ!" I screamed as I came to the surface, gasping for air and dog-paddling to the edge of the pool. One of the river safety guys yanked me from the water and asked if I was all right. "Yeah," I told him. "I'm fine."

I had flunked my first attempt at a true flyfishing stunt. Luckily John Bailey was able to find the weighted bottle. It had caught itself in a crack between two rocks. He was able to trace the fly line and retrieve the $1,500 custom rig intact.

The mistake I made ended up being exactly what the editor needed to give the sequence more suspense. As it turned out, the shot where I hit the wave and disappeared was used in the final cut where they decided to show Brad Pitt's character being submerged underneath the water. Like me, the character disappears for several seconds while everyone wonders if he will pop back up or not. Ever since my pitch in Redford's trailer, we hadn't been able to come up with a good idea for the actual swimming part of the scene. Now, by accident, we had it. The other takes went more smoothly, and were used to intercut with the close-ups of Brad as he swam the rapid.

In a special outdoor issue of *Esquire* Magazine just before the film was released 18 months later, I saw three photographs that were taken of me from a distance while I did the stunt. The caption read, "Brad Pitt swims the river while playing a fish in " '*A River Runs Through It*.' " I guess it's not all bad to be confused for the sexiest man alive.

Chapter Seven
The Catch & Release Ethic and Handling Fish

*I*n the film *"A River Runs Through It,"* you'll notice that there are rarely any scenes showing the fishermen killing their catch. But if you read the book, you'll know that a successful fishing trip for Paul, Norman, and the Reverend Maclean meant three full creels. In that manner, the juxtaposition between the book and the movie shows the evolution of the catch-and-release ethic in flyfishing. In the early days of flyfishing, with few fishermen and rivers full of fish, the practice of killing fish was fine. But with the ever-increasing popularity of flyfishing, shrinking habitat, parasites like whirling disease, the constant environmental threats of warming waters, increased water diversions for development, and the ever-present threat of more pollution, the last thing a trout needs to worry about is whether you're going to bonk him on the head to take him home and let him get freezer-burned. This sensitivity was reflected in the 1990's ethic of the movie, which doesn't show the fish being killed, versus the "three full creels" ethic of the 1920's.

Nowadays, the great majority of serious fishermen look seriously askance at the idea of killing fish. You will soon learn how efficient a good flyfisherman can be at hooking and landing fish, and it's not uncommon for a good flyfisherman to have 30- and 40-fish days. If he were to keep only five or six fish each day that he fished, one fisherman could make a fairly dramatic impact in a summer of fishing his local waters. Now think about all the other guys and gals out there, and you'll understand why we release the fish that we catch. Besides, as the great Lee Wulff once said, "A trout is far too beautiful to be caught only once."

In the previous chapter, we guided you through the process of hooking, playing and netting a trout. Now you need to learn how to release one. On the face of it, releasing a trout sounds very simple, but it can be difficult and frustrating. There is a right way to do it and there is most definitely a wrong way. First, it must be understood that, despite the harsh environment in which they live, trout are a delicate creature and cannot sustain much abuse.

A Fish Out of Water

We were once fishing on the Bighorn River and watched a pair of fishermen as they floated past in a dory. One of the fishermen hooked a nice rainbow and played it to the boat, whereupon he hoisted the fish into the bottom of the boat, grabbed it with dry hands, and proceeded to gesticulate to his partner, telling a story and laughing, while still holding the fish aloft with an iron grip. After the story was finished and the punch line was enjoyed, he bumbled around a few moments before he finally located his tape measure, and the fish was laboriously measured. Still not finished, the "angler" dug around for his camera, and the photo shoot began. Twenty seconds or so later, he wrenched the fly from the trout's jaws and tossed the fish back into the river, kerplunk! The whole process took at least two minutes.

We promise you, that rainbow was a dead trout. In the bar that evening, the fisherman began bragging about his catch, and we let the fisherman know how we felt in no uncertain terms.

The best way to release a trout is to bring him in quietly and remove the hook without touching him or removing him from the water. A very skilled fisherman often doesn't even use a net and can release a trout without even touching it. For a beginner, however, that's very difficult to do, so we're going to assume that you're going to use a net and handle fish. There are several maxims to releasing a trout successfully, and we hope you take them to heart.

There has been a large body of scientific study on successful techniques for releasing trout, and one rule is almost universally accepted: *no more than 30 seconds.* If a trout is held out of the water for more than 30 seconds, its chances for survival decrease radically. Think about it: if trout were angling for people, and bragging rights for trout were measured by taking photographs of people, how long would you want to be held underwater to have your picture taken? Ten seconds or two minutes? Thirty seconds is a pretty long time for most people to hold their breath underwater, and it's the same for trout.

Netting and Handling

Then, we must answer the question: use a net or not? As we said before, we recommend that beginners use a net. Once you really start getting the technique of catch-and-release down, then you can try landing fish without a net. Choose your net carefully, however. Don't use a cheap net with rough knots in it. Use a soft, smooth catch-and-release net that won't damage a trout's delicate skin.

The next rule for a trout's survival is to stay slimy. In other words, the trout is protected from infection and disease by a thin layer of mucous. **Wet your hands before touching a trout.** If you neglect to wet your hands and anything else that might come in contact with a fish before touching a trout, that slime will come off on your hands and you'll greatly decrease the trout's chances for long-term survival. In fact, we've seen trout with fungus on their sides in the shape of a handprint. But don't stop at your hands. Wet your net before you land a fish; if you're going to press him against your leg to remove a hook, make sure your waders are wet. If it's very cold and you must wear gloves, make sure they're plenty wet before you handle a fish. If at all possible, do not remove the fish from the water at all while releasing him.

Once you've got a fish in the net and your hands are wet, sometimes they're tough to handle. They'll flop around in the net and do everything they can to make the process difficult. Try to gently grasp the trout around his "shoulders," and be very careful not to press on his internal organs. The internal organs of a trout are very delicate. With very large fish, it has even been shown that simply removing a heavy fish from the water can damage his internal organs by removing the support that flotation provides. If the trout is very lively, sometimes turning him upside down will quiet a fish, making hook removal easier. Above all, do your best to **keep the fish in the water**. Sometimes we'll see people engrossed in delicately removing a hook, and they'll forget that they haven't let the fish breathe for a minute or more.

Hook Removal

That brings us to the most difficult part of the whole process: hook removal. The way to make hook removal easiest begins long before you've even hooked the trout. *Use barbless hooks.* You don't need to look for special barbless flies in the fly shop. Just remember to bend the barb flat with a small pliers or a surgeon's forceps before you even tie the hook on. Believe us, it will make life much, much easier. Often the hook just slips out once you slacken the tension on the line. You'll find out sometime how important barbless hooks are when you forget to bend down a barb. A barbed hook can really tear the tissue of a trout's mouth, no matter how skilled the fisherman is at releasing fish. Another important consideration, especially for beginning fishermen, is whether or not you'll be hooking yourself. Barbless hooks slip right out of a penetrated earlobe, fingertip or eyebrow, and a barbed hook can mean you go directly to the emergency room instead of finishing your trip down the river. Believe us, it happens.

Those are some of the "do's." Now for some of the "don't's" of releasing fish. Bass fishermen are fond of gripping a bass by its lower lip to momentarily paralyze it. For trout fishing, this is particularly bad form. It is damaging to a trout. Even more importantly, *never touch the gills of a trout.* The gills are extremely sensitive, and one poke of a finger can cause them to hemorrhage. Trout do not have a coagulant in their blood, so once a trout starts bleeding, he'll likely bleed to death. In fact, fish biologists estimate that the survival rate for a trout bleeding from the gills is only 10%. If the local regulations allow, the trout that's bleeding copiously is the trout to keep for supper.

The great majority of the fish you'll catch will be hooked in the jaws or lips and the flies will be easy to remove. But every now and then you'll land a trout and discover that your hook is imbedded deep in his throat or gills. This literally calls for special surgery, and that's why most good fishermen keep a pair of surgeon's forceps handy. They're great for removing flies from those tricky spots. With a little patience, a steady hand and particularly a barbless hook, it's possible to remove flies deeply imbedded down a trout's throat. Just keep in mind that you should try to remove the hook via the same direction it went in. Don't try to force it or rip it out. Sometimes it takes a little analysis before you figure out just how the hook went in. Trout often twist and wind the hooks and tippet into interesting configurations. Once you figure it out, the hooks are usually easy to remove.

The forceps are relatively inexpensive—less than $10 at most fly shops—and they help you feel good about releasing your fish. If a hook is particularly deep in a trout's gullet or twisted into its lip, any errant poke with a forceps may cause him to gush blood, so that may be the time to simply clip off the leader as close as you can and leave the fly in there. Eventually it'll work its way free and rust away to nothing.

Resuscitation

Once the fly is removed, the trout isn't "out of the woods" yet. You still must make sure that he swims away under his own power. Most of the time, the fish will let you know when they're ready to go. Once they sense freedom, they'll zip away for the depths of the pool. But occasionally the fight will drag on, or the removal of the fly is taxing to the fish, and you'll find yourself holding a trout that's struggling to survive. You can resuscitate a trout by gently supporting his belly and facing him into a gentle current while using his tail as a handle to push and pull him gently through the water. This action will force oxygen-bearing water through his gills to revive him. Sometimes it might take ten or fifteen minutes to revive a trout, after which it's best to let him slide over into a calm spot to revive further. If he goes belly up, however, he's as good as dead, so watch him carefully.

One factor in a trout's survival is how well and how long you played him. If you dragged him back and forth for fifteen minutes and took two minutes to remove the hook, his chances are much worse than if the fight took two minutes and the release took ten seconds. The longer you play a fish, the more lactic acid builds up in its muscles, and the lower the chances of survival. When you're playing a fish, you may want to get all the thrill out of it that you can, but there will be more fish to catch. Bring him on in and release him quickly, and he'll stand a much better chance of surviving. We find that most beginners really don't know how much pressure they can bring to bear on a trout with a fly rod. Actually, it's quite a lot. The more pressure you put on the fish, the quicker he comes to the net, the release goes faster, and the fish swims away healthy. Use the strength of the rod to tire the fish as quickly as possible.

Releasing

Note that we said "catch and release" when we talk about releasing fish. We didn't say "throw them back." We've all seen some fisherman who catches a fish, grabs it roughly by the lip, squeezes it with a dry hand until he's ripped the hook out, and then throws the fish back in the water from chest height. That's what you call a dead fish. If you see someone treating fish roughly, gently offer to give them a few pointers on releasing fish. It really does make a difference. In the hands of a good flyfisherman, a trout will spend only seconds before being released, sometimes with the fisherman never touching the fish and the fish never leaving the water.

If you're going to take to the river with a fly rod in hand, you must acknowledge that, once you hook a fish, you have to decide what you want to do with that fish: release it or kill it. There is no in-between. Either the release must be accomplished efficiently and humanely, or the kill must happen the same way. We hate to see mangled fish swimming around lethargically, struggling to maintain their equilibrium in the current, simply because some yahoo bungled the job of releasing them. If you're going to do the job, learn to do it well. Do it right.

Keeping Trout

Of course, there are a few times and places where it's entirely appropriate to keep a few fish according to the local regulations. If you're at a deserted lake teeming with trout, or a little stream chock full of brookies, go ahead and keep a couple for supper. But you shouldn't plan on making trout the mainstay of your diet now that you've got the basics of flyfishing, and by all means don't cave in to the hungry hordes at home who say, "Make sure you bring home enough to feed all of us!" They can go to the store or to Happyjack's Fish Farm if they want fish that badly.

On rare occasions friends or relatives will ask to go fishing with us and they'll insist on keeping their limit of fish. That's their legal right. (Our guide clients don't enjoy that privilege. We fish strictly catch-and-release.) They've bought the license and legally they're entitled to take a certain number of fish home. But we feel that if they want to eat fish so badly, they can do the killing themselves. It's funny how many people lose their appetite for fish when they're faced with the task of smacking a beautiful trout on the head with a stick. More often than not, that fish ends up swimming away. Then our friends experience the beauty of knowing that trout is still there in the river for another day of flyfishing.

Letting Them Go

by Gary Hubbell

I can still remember it like it was yesterday. I was fifteen years old, working a summer job for the school keeping the lawns green during the day and fishing all I could in the evenings. One night, as the sun slipped behind the ridge, my father and I were lacing on our old tennis shoes to go fishing. We seldom left the house until the sun was on its way down, because the hatches often occur on the Roaring Fork right at dusk. When the light gets golden, the river emanates a cool swampy smell, a smell of life and richness. I love that smell. It smells like flyfishing.

As we rigged up our rods and prepared to leave, I said, "Dad, why don't we release everything we catch tonight?" My father gave me a stunned look. "Are you kidding?" he said. "Don't you like to eat fish?"

"Well, yeah," I stammered, "but we've got a lot of fish in the freezer, and Mom never cooks them anyway. I think if we let more fish go, the fishing would be better around here."

Dad mulled the idea for a few moments. "Okay," he agreed. "Whatever you say." I was elated. My father was a traditional son of the West, which is to say that he recognized natural resources and was ready to use them. He had grown up in western Kansas during the last years of the Depression, and he had many stories about living poor. My grandfather had once started walking to town with a rifle and a box of 50 .22 cartridges, and reached town with 51 jackrabbit skins. You see, rabbit pelts brought five cents each, and that was a good bit of money for one walk to town. He had killed the last two rabbits sitting together with one shot. My grandmother had picked and cooked wild horseradish to sell in town for five cents a quart, and even in the days of my youth she still liked to walk along ditchbanks looking for wild asparagus and rhubarb.

In our home, we heated with firewood, ate vegetables from the garden and venison from the hills, and I had been contributing stringers of fish to the table since I was six years old. By the time I was 15, I had killed several hundred fish, and had shot a couple of deer that were appreciated additions to the menu. Our ethic was no different than anyone else's in town. When you went fishing, you went to catch your limit of eight trout, by God, and there was even a small sense of failure if you didn't manage to accomplish that. The conversation at the barber shop typically went something like, "Howdy, Fred, watcha been up to?"

"Aw, not much. Went fishing yesterday."

"Didja get your limit?"

My suggestion to release the trout we were going to catch that night was against all the tenets of my family's upbringing. There was only one reason to release our fish, and that was waste. There was no reason to kill more until we had eaten the trout we had in the freezer.

However, I had noticed that the fishing wasn't as good as it should be. There were holes where only the occasional trout was rising during a good hatch. The fish were getting ever smaller, until it was uncommon to catch a trout over 13 or 14 inches. And, to be honest, I was tired of killing fish. I had reached a point where it no longer mattered to bring home a mess of fish. I was just as happy to know that the trout I caught were still in the river.

That night I chose to fish in shorts. It was a warm summer evening, and I didn't see the point in getting my jeans wet—neither of us owned a set of waders. Dad and I worked our way up to our favorite hole, the sun slipping behind the mountain. Caddis were hatching. For visibility, I tied on a Yellow Humpy. We both started casting. Dad hooked a German brown, too small to consider killing, and he winked at me as he released it. "We'll let him grow a little," he chuckled.

I hooked a nice German brown and played it to the net. "That one's pan sized," Dad goaded me. I removed the hook and slipped it back into the water without comment. I looked back at Dad and started casting again. He laughed.

We each caught several more fish, but nothing of any consequence. We released them all. The hatch was rolling now, and there were fish rising. It was getting dark. I waded deeper, the cold water getting very close to my...ah, upper thighs. My feet found a large rock underwater, and I perched on it, using it as a casting platform. I saw a large fish rising close to the far bank, a long cast away. I peeled out more line and cast to him. I was eagerly anticipating the strike, and sure enough, it came. I set the hook so hard that my feet slipped out from under me and I tumbled into the waist-deep water. I was submerged for a moment in the cold water; my hat was floating away, and I snatched it with my free hand. But lo and behold, I had kept the line tight, and the fish was still on. Out of my peripheral vision, I could see my father convulsing with laughter.

It was a beautiful fish, and a nice long fight. I played him well. When he came to the net, Dad marveled at the solid slab of wild trout. He was still having trouble with the idea of catch and release—this was a nice two-pound rainbow. I admired him for a moment, then slipped him back into the water. I looked up at my father. "Good job," he said.

That night, I discovered a new feeling from flyfishing, an elation, a joy that I had connected with a wild being. I had won our battle, but the trout was still in the river, ready to be challenged again on another day. Never before would I have released a 16-inch rainbow. Now that I had, the tables were forever turned. Ever since that golden summer evening, I find it remarkable that I once used to kill fish.

Chapter Eight
Fly Selection

"*F*lyfishing." That term in itself implies that you're going to be fishing with—well, a fly. Practically every flyfisherman has been asked, at one time or another, if that means that we tie insects onto hooks and fish with them. No, it doesn't, but the concept is close.

The term started out defining the limited concept of catching fish on a hook that had been wrapped with feathers and hair to imitate an insect, but from the world of bait fishing, anglers knew that trout eat many other things. So when fly tyers began making imitations of grasshoppers, mice, minnows and fish eggs, for example, those imitations are also called "flies." The same goes for the brilliant eight-inch minnow imitations used for tarpon fishing. Of course, they do not imitate insect life, but they're tied with fur and feathers, and are fished with a fly rod, so they're called "tarpon flies."

For purposes of definition, there are basically four different kinds of flies: 1) **Dry flies** are imitations of adult aquatic insects that are designed to float on top of the water; 2) **Nymphs**, which are imitations of sub-surface, immature aquatic insects in the larvae or pupae stage of development; 3) **Terrestrials**, which are practically any insect or creature that exists outside the river, such as beetles, ants, grasshoppers, mice, etc.; and 4) **Streamers**, which are imitations of a minnows, leeches, sculpins, or any other swimming creature such as a frog or crayfish. Streamers are often purely an attractor pattern of brightly colored feathers that don't really imitate anything in particular, but are designed to provoke a fish's instinct to strike or protect its territory.

Flies are sized according to the size of the hook that they're tied on, and the bigger the number, the smaller the hook. A size 28 Griffith's Gnat is a very, very small midge pattern, so tiny that you wonder how anyone could have possibly tied it. On the opposite end, a #2 streamer is tied on a huge hook, close to two inches long. But the size of the hook has nothing to do with the size of the fish you can catch on it. There are many trout weighing over five pounds caught every year on #24 hooks and smaller.

Names

Flies are named according to the whim of the tyer and what he's trying to imitate. For example, a "LaFontaine caddis pupae emerger" means that the pattern was designed by Gary LaFontaine to imitate the caddis pupae as it is hatching from its pupal shuck and emerging to the surface of the river. The name tells you quite a bit. An "Ausable Wulff" is an attractor pattern designed by Lee Wulff specifically for the Ausable River in Michigan. Sometimes the flies will bear the Latin name of the insect that they are supposed to imitate, like the "Baetis" mayfly or "Pteronarcys" stonefly. More likely flies will carry the common name of the insect or perhaps a description of the materials used to tie them, like an "Elk Hair Caddis," or a "Brown Hackle Peacock." The names of flies are as varied and colorful, boring and interesting as the men and women who designed and tied them.

But it is by no means necessary to even begin to know the names and uses of all the flies out there. There are literally thousands. For a beginner, figuring out which fly to use can be an intimidating process. Where do you begin? First, there are a few mainstay patterns which can be used to catch trout on practically any river, and your local fly shop will be glad to show you which ones work the best on your local rivers.

Matching the Hatch

Your most important tool for fly selection, however, is your power of observation. It really isn't necessary for a beginner to know all the names of the flies in his box. What is essential, however, is to start the thought process. As flyfishermen, we call it "matching the hatch." In short, we want to throw a fly that imitates what the fish are eating. For example, let's assume that you've tugged on your waders, walked down to the river, you've put a new leader on your fly line and you're ready to rig up your rod.

But first you have many questions to answer. Look at the river. Do you see any activity on the surface? Are there bugs fluttering around? Do you see fish rising to eat these bugs? What color are they? How big are they? What do their wings look like? Do you have a fly in your box that resembles them? You reach into the river and bring up a rock. What kind of nymphs do you see there? Big ones? Little ones? Do they look ready to hatch—are their wing cases bulging? What time of year is it? Have you seen hatches there at this time last year? What were they? What was happening on the river yesterday? Two days ago? Last week?

As you can see, this manner of flow-chart thinking leads you ever closer to the decision you should make about which fly to use and how to fish it. There are "yes" and "no" answers that make the decision easy. For example, you don't see any activity on the river. There are very few insects fluttering around. You don't see any fish rising. Hmmm. Maybe it's not a good idea to throw a dry fly. Maybe you should try a nymph. So you reach into the river, dredge up a melon-sized rock, and it's clustered with caddis cases, several smaller nymphs, and Oh! There are three big fat stonefly nymphs scurrying around on the rock. You look in your box, and you have a stonefly nymph pattern that's really a close imitation of what these guys look like. It would be an excellent choice to nymph with that stonefly pattern.

Now let's assume it goes pretty well for you. You get three or four very obvious strikes in the first half-hour or so, you catch a couple of fish, and for the next two hours you're very entertained. Action is good on the stonefly nymph, and you're proud of yourself for having made the choice to use it. Well and good. But after a while the sun goes behind a cloud, the action really starts to slow down on the stonefly, and you notice there are a lot more insects fluttering about on the surface of the water. You notice a trout rising, in fact right where you had just been fishing and didn't get any strikes. Hmmm. Guess he didn't want the stonefly, did he? What's he eating? It looks like a little dun-colored insect with fine gossamer wings. One flutters by and you catch it in your hand. Yes. It's got an upswept wing that looks like a sail, three very fine strands of tail, and a dun-yellow body about 3/8-inch long.

As you look in your dry fly box, you notice out of your peripheral vision that still more insects are hatching, and the surface of the river is starting to liven with trout rising. Yes! You locate just the fly, what the guy at the shop said was a size 14 Pale Morning Dun. You remove the stonefly nymph, the weight, and the strike indicator, tie on the dry fly, grease it up with some dry fly floatant, and in a minute, you've gotten your first strike on a dry fly. You've matched the hatch.

That is how the fly selection process works. It is absolutely integral with your powers of observation and your thinking process. Of course, sometimes it's not that easy. Sometimes you feel like you can't buy a thrill, like all the fish in the river are dead, like there never were insects or fish in the river at all. But usually you can catch fish if you open your eyes, notice what's going on, and follow your hunch.

Other Factors

There are other factors of fly selection that fishermen know from experience. For example, it is widely known among trout fishermen that German browns spawn in the fall, and that they become much more aggressive and territorial when spawning season nears. Therefore, it's a good bet to put on a streamer and pulse the streamer across a big pool. When a big brown strikes that streamer, he'll hit it like a truck, mostly out of irritation and aggression.

Conversely, rainbows spawn in the spring, and that's when you can trigger their territorial instinct by pulling a streamer through their domain. Or there will be natural factors that, through observation, you can make a hypothesis and an experiment. If it rained hard the night before and the water is murky, it stands to reason that a lot of sediment has been washed into the river. It's also much harder for the fish to see your fly. So why not try a San

Juan worm, a red "fly" that looks like it's been tied from a pipe cleaner. Some snobs may look down their noses at your manner of "matching the hatch", but you'll catch fish when others won't.

Or how about the times when you hike into a high-country lake during the summer? It's well known amongst the small fraternity of high-country lake fishermen that flying ants hatch out of ant colonies in profusion and seek to establish new colonies. When the wind picks up in the afternoon, a flying ant pattern can be deadly on an alpine lake.

Other times it's necessary to simply be different. On the Roaring Fork, we have what we call the "Mother's Day hatch," which is a huge caddis hatch that occurs every year around Mother's Day. At that time, so many caddis hatch at once that there are literally huge clouds of insects in the air. You can't drive down the highway without your windshield becoming smeared with bugs. Of course, the fish are gorging themselves sick. Everywhere they look, there's another caddis bumbling around, ready to be sucked up like a vacuum cleaner. Sometimes it actually gets discouraging to fish this hatch, because there are so many insects on the water that there's really no reason for a trout to take your Elk Hair Caddis, which, although it's a good pattern, it's still no substitute for the real thing. We know a good fisherman who ties on a Lime Trude, which is a very garish fly with a lime-green body and a white wing. It is nothing like an Elk Hair Caddis, but he seems to catch a lot of fish, simply because the fly is different than anything else.

That's why attractor patterns work. There are many flies in a fisherman's box that imitate an insect very precisely, down to the little antennae and the tails of the insect. But there are a great many others that don't imitate anything at all; they're just bold, colorful patterns that happen to catch fish. Some of the flies in this category are the Royal Coachman, the Royal Wulff, the H&L Variant, the Humpy, the Pink Lady, the Prince Nymph, and the Rio Grande King. Go into a fly shop sometime and look for these names. These flies feature bright white wings, red thoraxes, bushy tails, and dark bodies. None of them imitate anything in nature specifically, but all of them imitate something in nature generally. That's why they work. A Prince Nymph, with its white wings and dark body, generally imitates a caddis larvae. A Humpy is a fair approximation of an adult caddis.

Usually attractor patterns are best used in fast, tumbling "pocket water," where the fish are concentrated in little pools behind boulders and logs. Throw an H&L Variant into a pocket of fast, clear water that holds trout, and you'll likely get a strike. Sometimes the attractor patterns actually work better than the imitation of the insect that's hatching at the time. Another use for attractor patterns is as a "marker fly," which is when we tie two flies on the same leader: one that imitates the insects that are hatching (and is typically very hard to see), and the other is a bright, very visible attractor pattern tied about 18 inches apart. This technique enables the angler to easily locate his flies, and when there's a strike, he can spot the take and set the hook.

Fly selection is one of the things that makes flyfishing so much fun. It allows every angler to ponder, to speculate, to hypothesize and follow your own hunch. And what works for one fisherman may not work for another. Sometimes when two or three of us go fishing together, we all find ourselves fishing different flies and we're all catching fish. Sometimes only one fly will work, and nothing else will do. However, if you're going to be a good flyfisherman, your brain has to be engaged. You must observe the processes of nature taking place around you, and make your choices of patterns to use based on your observations. In the process, you'll learn a lot more about nature in general, and you'll take that knowledge home with you. It's a satisfying feeling. It takes a thinker to be a flyfisherman, and that's one of the ways that flyfishing will hook you.

It's Your Choice

by Gary Hubbell

Fly selection is one of those things that truly shows our individual personalities as flyfishermen. Fly selection shows the difference between such widely divergent traits as boldness and caution, extravagance, stubbornness, intuition, ignorance, belief, and even physical strength or frailty.

Which fly you choose to tie on your line is entirely your decision. Whatever you decide, it's certain that your friends will be interested in your choice. If they're catching more fish than you are, they'll likely offer advice as to which fly to use. If you're catching more than they are, you can expect an inquiry as to which fly is bringing you success. Often fly selection can be the most intriguing decision you'll make all day.

Many folks get very scientific about their fly selection. They'll pull out a screen and scuffle bugs off the bottom, then match them in the most minute details. If you've met my co-author, John Dietsch, you'll know that he fits this description. He fusses about little details, and sometimes he's too exacting.

But, as I showed him one Montana evening, fly selection doesn't have to be so precise. John and I were fishing on DePuy's Spring Creek near Livingston after a long day of filming fishing sequences for *"The ESPN Flyfishing School."* It was my first time fishing the hallowed Montana spring creek, but John had been fishing it for years and had promised to show me the ropes. John had explained to me that DePuy's was one of the most sophisticated small-bug "match the hatch" rivers in the world, and the fish were extremely selective. "If you don't have the right fly, forget it," John warned.

By the time we got to the water it was almost dark, so dark in fact that it was difficult to tie a knot without a flashlight. There was a huge hatch going on, and fish were boiling on the surface in loud splashy rises. John was trying to catch the bugs as they flew past, then match them exactly to the flies in his box. In the failing light, he couldn't decide between a size 18 Pale Morning Dun and a size 18 Red Quill.

I used a different tactic. I felt a strange sensation from time to time, that of fluttering wings brushing my face. They felt rather large, like a size 10. I couldn't see what it was, but I knew it had to be big bugs hatching. From the sound of the splashes, I knew the fish couldn't be that excited about the little mayflies John was seeing. The sound of the rises meant, to me, that the fish were feeding on something large, so I tied on a size 10 H&L Variant (see Chapter 10 Sidebar) because of its size and very visible white wings.

Soon I was hooking fish after fish, and big ones, too. John's luck wasn't nearly as good. Finally he forgot his pride and asked, with a tone of frustration in his voice, "What in the hell are you using, Hubbell?"

"A size 10 H&L Variant, " I replied, releasing another fish in the cool Montana spring water.

"An H&L Variant? No way. You're joking."

"I'm as serious as a heart attack," I said, hooking another thrashing trout.

"Jesus," John said. "Why an H&L Variant? That's not what's hatching."

"All I know, John," I explained, my reel whirring, "is that something big keeps coming up and hitting me in the face."

(He's lying. He's a fisherman. But it makes a great story, doesn't it? J.D.)

Chapter Nine
Reading Water and Approaching Fish

When approaching a river, it's important to remember that your presence is frightening to a fish, so you need to move slowly, quietly, and keep a low profile. Bright colors, loud voices, kicking rocks around on the bottom—these are sure ways to spook fish. We've known many beginners who thought flyfishing is just a lark, a way to play in the water for a day. No. It's serious— serious fun, that is. If you want to catch fish, you have to rediscover some predatory instincts. Even if you intend to release a fish, you intend to capture him, and that means stalking and catching that fish. You are the predator, and the fish are aware of that.

First and foremost, when you approach a river, stop and look before you wade right in. Often there will be fish congregated in the calm water near the banks, and many beginners never even know that they spook these fish away. Observe what's happening on the river. Take the time to look for rising fish, hatching insects, swallows flying above the water, and other indicators. Turn over some rocks underwater and look at the insects clustered there. Then choose a fly and slip into the stream.

Typically, the best way to approach a fish is from downstream, casting upstream, and there are two good reasons for that. First, fish normally face upstream. That's how they maintain their position in the current best, and that's how their food comes to them— floating downstream on the current. Fish don't see well behind them, so you have a better chance of sneaking up on them from behind. Second, as you walk in the river, you will muddy the water, kicking up sand, dirt, leaves and such. A wary fish knows what this disturbance means, and he's going to be moving away from it. You want to fish undisturbed water. There are downstream casting techniques, but we'll save those for a more advanced book.

If it's a bright day, do yourself a favor and bring a pair of polarized sunglasses. The polarized lenses screen most of the glare and reflection from the surface of the water, enabling you to see into the water, sometimes with great clarity. That way you can see the structure, currents, and sometimes even the fish in the water. A $10 pair of polarized glasses can bring a lot of truths about the river to light.

Structure

When looking at a river, there is a basic principle to keep in mind: fish are like you—they will choose the path of least resistance. In other words, when you look at the river, you can imagine places where you could comfortably withstand the tugging force of the current: behind that rock, downstream of that pile of driftwood, underneath a tree root poking into the water, or in the little slot where the two currents meet. The fish feel the same way. If the current is too strong, they are unable to maintain their position in the river. They won't be holding in the middle of a rapid or in a strong, rushing current, or right below a pounding waterfall.

When you're reading water, however, you're not just looking at structures in the water, but you must also keep the needs of the fish in mind. Trout need oxygen and a ready food source in addition to cover. And, a trout's needs may change according to the seasons. For example, during spring runoff it may be most important that a fish simply find refuge from the torrent, so any little backwater is likely to hold fish. In the winter, it may be that the trout need deep, slow holding water. In the hot days of August, when the flows are lowest, they'll often be looking for oxygen, which they find where the water rolls over the rocks at the head of a riffle.

It's up to you to recognize those structures in the water, and then engage your brain to figure out what the fish need and where they might be. At first, the river may seem to be a rushing cacophony of water, one spot indistinguishable from another. And, of course, some rivers are much easier to read than others, where the fast spots are really fast and the calm spots are very calm. Other rivers are much more subtle, requiring a practiced eye to differentiate between spots likely to hold fish and those that aren't. Without going into excessive detail, we've defined some categories of structures in the water that are likely to hold fish.

Riffles

A riffle is where the current rolls over a rocky bar and then slows down. Riffles are characterized by broken water, and as such, riffles are a good source of oxygen. Often the head of a riffle, or the upstream part, is whitewater, and it takes a strong fish to hold his position there. The very nature of a riffle means that the bottom is rough. The rocks that create the waves also provide a small slot of cover, so you'll find fish where you wouldn't think it is possible. When nymphing, the trick is to really load up on weight and get your drift down to the bottom. You'll be amazed at how many fish you hook up. Otherwise, you'll find trout further down in a riffle, where the current slows down and there are calm spots for the trout to hold.

Riffles are great fun to fish, because they're usually easy to read and easy to approach. The turbulence of the water makes the fish feel secure from predators, and it also makes it easy for you to get near. When fishing a riffle, start out near the bottom and work your way up. It may take a couple of hours to work a riffle thoroughly, and they can be very engrossing. Take note that the biggest fish are typically found near the head of a riffle, because they're strong enough to withstand the current and they can also muscle out the smaller fish. The best feeding position is at the head of the riffle because those trout get first crack at any insects floating by.

If the riffle occurs where there is a bend in the river, there will be calmer water on the inside of the bend, and often you'll find more fish in that calmer water. If you're nymphing while fishing a riffle, you may find that you have to add weight as you move towards the head of it, so that your fly will drift close to the bottom. Dry flies are best drifted in the calmer spots of a riffle, where fish are feeding on terrestrials and emerging insects.

Runs

A run is a smooth, deep glide of water that usually follows a riffle. The water may occasionally boil from large underwater obstructions, but generally runs are quiet. However, the current is often fairly swift in a run. Big fish will hold on the bottom of a run, because they feel protected in the deep, cool water, and they have a good chance at small prey like minnows and crawfish, as well as big mayflies and stoneflies.

When approaching a run, you must be more careful than while approaching a riffle. It's easier for trout to see you and hear you. Often trout will use runs and riffles as a bedroom and dining room—holding in the run when insect activity is low, and moving up into the riffle to feed when the insects are active. Runs are great spots to fish a dry fly during an active hatch, because the fly is easily spotted but the current keeps the line moving and the fish tolerate a little imprecision on a beginner's part.

Pools

A pool is a deep, slow "hole" where big trout like to hang out. The water is very still in a pool, so the fish don't have to use much energy to maintain their position. The trout usually have the advantage in a pool, because the still water transmits practically every vibration and sound. Trout like the dark depths of a pool during the daytime, and often come up in the evenings for hatches. Sometimes pools are connected in a sequence with riffles and runs, providing crucial winter holding cover for trout. In fact, you can almost tell if a river is going to be a good fishery by the riffle:pool ratio. Ideally, the ratio of riffles to pools should be 1:1. If a freestone river has many more riffles than pools—say three or four riffles for each pool—it won't provide enough of the crucial winter holding water that enables fish to survive year-round.

Eddies and Seams

Anyone who has paddled a kayak or a canoe down a river will know about an eddy. An eddy is where the current switches directions and goes backwards. Eddies are usually caused when the current, running close to the bank, is forced to overcome an obstruction. The obstruction causes a calm spot next to the bank, and when the current is pulled back into that calm spot, an eddy is created. A true eddy is difficult to fish, because the water reverses direction and this makes getting a good drift almost impossible. But when there is simply a calm spot right next to a faster current, it's a good bet that there are fish in there. Not only is there refuge from the current, but there is a steady food source right nearby, as nymphs are swept past in the current. A trout that has found a position in a nice eddy can pick and choose when he wants to feed.

A back eddy provides one of the rare places where a fish faces downstream, because the current reverses itself. The food comes toward a fish when he faces into the current, which in this case is downriver.

A seam is a calm spot caused by an obstruction in the river such as a rock or log. Directly downstream of the obstruction, the current is slowed significantly, and you'll find that trout love these slots in the current. Of all the features in the current, seams are perhaps the easiest to spot. They're also fairly easy to approach, because the water surrounding them is typically rough and fast, hiding your approach. Seams are great for nymph fishing, because the weight and the flies are easily drifted, but they can also offer great dry fly fishing for a precision cast.

Undercut Banks

Another good holding spot for trout is under a riverbank that has been gouged out by the current. Often there will be a network of tree roots that hold the bank together, even though it's hollowed out underneath. Trout love these cool, shady spots where they are invulnerable to predators from above, they have a steady food supply flowing by, and where all but the best fly casters can't seem to find a good drift. When wading, it can be difficult to fish an undercut bank, because there is often a swift tongue of current down the middle of a deep run, with the undercut bank on the other side. You'll find yourself up to the top of your chest waders and still unable to get close enough.

One way to lure out a big trout from an undercut bank is to flash a streamer past his lair. Often that's the enticement he needs, and strikes can be crunching in those situations. Many anglers prefer to cast from dories, or drift boats, at these undercut banks, and as they float by, they may be able to hook up dozens of nice trout over the course of a day.

Merging Currents

A dead spot of calm water is created where two currents come together. Say, for example, there is an island in the middle of two swift currents. Downstream of the island, the two currents meet again, and the precise spot where they meet is called a seam. Fish are attracted to these merging currents because the conflicting currents cancel each other out and create a calm spot, and there is also a great deal of food drifting by. Merging currents are difficult to drift a dry fly because the cast must be absolutely precise, but they're easier to nymph.

Flats and Shallows

Flats are tricky to fish, because the water is so still, slow, and shallow that fish are very aware of any predator's approach. You must be very cautious when approaching a flat. Trout feel very vulnerable from all sides, and any splash or loud voice can spook the fish. There's only one reason for trout to hold in a flat, and that's to feed. When a good hatch is going on, the fish will gorge in the flats. Emerging insects are easy to spot, and the fish pick them off at will. An interesting phenomenon sometimes develops in the flats, where a group of trout form together in a pod and move through the flats as a group, feeding as they go.

As a flyfisherman, you have to be on top of your game to catch fish in the flats. Any presentation must be delicate. Any time your false cast slaps the water will be the end of your success in that spot. And because the trout's visibility is so great in the clear, slow water, your casts must be accurate at long distances. Long leaders are the rule when fishing flats, because you don't want to "line" a wary trout by drifting a thick fly line over his head. Nymph fishing, with its weight and strike indicators, is difficult in the flats. Sometimes your best cast in the flats is to cast downstream and actually pay out line to a feeding trout, so that your fly is the first thing he sees.

It's easy to lump all the features of a stream into different categories, but the truth is that every river, and every stretch of river, is different. You might find the features of a flat, a riffle, merging currents and an undercut bank all in a hundred feet of river. The most important thing (we'll stress it again) is to keep your eyes open. Take a close look at the river, try to figure out what the fish might need, and think about where they could be, and present a fly to them as best you can.

Preserving Life's Metaphors

by John Dietsch

"It is those we live with and love and should know who elude us."

—Norman Maclean
"A River Runs Through It"

As you become more experienced and begin discovering some of the profound truths about the river that we've discussed in this book, you will also begin to discover something else. You'll come to see just how fragile an environment the river ecosystem is. Whether it's mining, timber cutting, cattle ranching, or construction, if you're on the river with any frequency, you will notice how man profoundly affects a fishery over time.

And if you are like many flyfishermen, you will get involved to help conserve these precious cold-water fisheries. A good example is the Big Blackfoot where Norman Maclean and his brother fished in *"A River Runs Through It."* By the early 1990's the Blackfoot was hardly worth fishing because of serious environmental degradation that had gone unchecked for years. There were so many debris-causing clearcuts and so much mine waste in the river that Redford decided the river was useless for the film. Luckily, the attention the river received from the movie helped bring it back and today it is a testament to what people can do to help fisheries that have been damaged and neglected.

However, this kind of turnaround cannot take place without the support of the new breed of flyfishers who are coming into the fold. As fishing pressure increases across the world, the onus of conservation will increasingly fall upon the new generation of flyfishers to stand up for the rivers they love. The river is a special place that can never be replaced, a finite resource that we all need to protect.

"A River Runs Through It" is more than a great fishing story,

it's one of the greatest pieces of Western literature we have in the English language. I often wonder what would have happened if Norman and Paul had grown up on the Blackfoot of the 1980's when its trout population was at a record low. Maybe the Macleans would have given up on flyfishing and their story never would have been told. How can you have a story like that without fishing on the Blackfoot as a central metaphor? You can't.

I thought about this notion as my father and I sat on the porch of my brother's small house near San Francisco.

"Hey, look at this," my dad said, pointing to a headline in the *Chronicle*. "Salmon Spawning up Devil's Gulch. First Time in Ten Years."

"Where is that?" I asked with enthusiasm.

"Not far from here, it looks like."

Within minutes we were in the car and on the way to Devil's Gulch, a half-hour drive from the Golden Gate Bridge. What is left of salmon and steelhead runs in Bay Area streams have been protected for years, so this spontaneous expedition would simply be to sight fish, not catch them.

After spending the last several days of rain at my brother's bedside, it felt good to see the sun again. My dad, my brother and I had fished together most of our lives. We would have asked my brother to come along to search for fish, but this was one trip he could not take; my brother was dying of cancer.

We parked the car at the Devil's Gulch sign and walked up the small foot trail. Down below, the swollen creek roared as it cascaded over the boulders, forming a series of pools and runs. We kept walking, our eyes peeled for spawning salmon. After an hour of searching, night began to fall. The river seemed barren of life.

"We should turn around," my dad suggested. "It'll be dark going back."

"One more run," I said stubbornly as I hurried up the side of the creek. My dad followed me to a small waterfall.

"There," we said together. Sure enough, a 20-inch coho salmon washed over the waterfall. In the pool below, it tried to swim upstream, to keep itself steady, but its fins were too weak. By all the black markings and white fungus, it was evident that this salmon had already swam up from the ocean ten miles away. The valiant fish had spawned, and was now fighting a losing battle with mother nature.

We stood there in silence, watching the salmon struggle in the fading light of the gulch, surrounded by fern and dripping oaks. The current caught up with the fish and as hard as he kicked with his tail, the current gradually flushed him downstream until he disappeared around the bend.

Dad put his arm around me, and for a moment we both stared into the eddy of the pool in front of us.

"The circle of life," my dad said.

As we began walking down the trail, I began thinking how these streams were once packed solid with red and silver bodies. The Native American shamans used to have visions of these creatures swimming up the veins of the earth: "Shamans who lived in magic villages under the sea who disguised themselves as fish to visit the people of the river."

In the old days, the salmon died for a purpose: to give the river life. Their fragments of flesh fed their offspring and their bodies provided food for eagles, bears, and other animals...suddenly I began to see, as we walked down the trail in silence, that life is a circle. That with every death there is a birth, and that maybe the approaching death of my brother Kresser would not be an error or a sacrifice, but like the salmon, a poetic dance.

Three days later my brother died from cancer, but not before seeing his first child grown to be six months old. And just three hours before his death, my sister gave birth to a baby girl in Oakland. My father witnessed the birth of his grandchild and the death of his son in the same day. Just as the salmon die to give the rivers life, so it seems, my brother died as part of a mystical song to the roundness of life.

Chapter Ten
Fly Tying

*I*f you go to a fly shop and buy a selection of flies for the day at close to two dollars each, you figure out right away that tying flies might be a good idea. Flies are expensive, and some of them are very simple. A good tyer can whip out a dozen Prince Nymphs in twenty minutes, so looking at it simply from an economic perspective, it makes sense to tie your own flies.

However, fly tying can bring more satisfaction than simply saving a few bucks. The feeling of catching a trout on a fly you've tied yourself is very rewarding. It's no longer a matter of just catching a fish, but catching a fish on your own creation. Personally, both of us can buy flies at wholesale prices of less than a dollar each, and we're busy guys, so it doesn't make sense for us to sit down and tie Royal Wulffs all evening and wake up with a sore neck.

But we still appreciate great fly tyers, and many is the time that we've been frustrated with our fly selection. Sometimes you just can't find a pattern that imitates the phenomenon that you're seeing on the water. A good tyer will look closely at what's happening with a particular insect, and he'll go home and tie up a new pattern, then come to the river the next day and experiment with it. Some tyers will even tie up an imitation right on the river.

Like anything, fly tying can be taken to extremes. We have a neighbor who ties a size 20 mayfly pattern that is simply exquisite. He goes so far as to separate the filaments of a pheasant tail feather and braid them in three separate strands to create a lifelike tail for the fly. This work requires a jeweler's magnifying lamp and tiny tweezers, and chances are he'll lose most of them on a streamside bush or an underwater rock. But he'll also catch fish with them. We know another fellow who slams on the brakes when he spots an interesting bit of roadkill. He'll experiment with the feathers and fur of almost anything, but he and his tying bench were banished to the woodshed by his wife, who didn't care for the odors of some of his prizes.

There's also a protocol regarding the patenting of new fly patterns, whereby the originator of a particular design is given the honor of naming his creation and the tyer may even receive royalties if a distributor starts selling quantities of it.

In fact, if you want your name to live on forever, design a can't-miss fly pattern and name it after yourself. The Griffith's Gnat, the Royal Wulff, and the Light Cahill are all examples of this.

Materials and Tools

Materials used in fly tying are as interesting as the names of the flies. They range from the everyday, such as thread and wire, to the exotic, such as impala, to the space-age, such as mylar. It's helpful to be a hunter. Gary collects pheasant tails, hare's masks, elk hair, duck feathers, goose quills and grouse feathers on his autumn hunting expeditions. Many tyers will trade a few dozen flies for a batch of good materials. Other fellows with the ability to keep birds find pleasure in raising roosters with the desired thin feathers on their capes that produce good hackles for dry flies. Again, it brings satisfaction as well as significant savings when you can find your own fly tying materials. Otherwise, your eyes will pop when you learn that the fly shop wants a hundred bucks for that premium rooster cape or five bucks for that little patch of elk hide with the hair on. It's easy to spend a good chunk of money on fly tying materials.

If you decide you want to try fly tying, the best way is to take a class from the local fly shop or from a community college. Don't just rush into a fly shop and buy five hundred bucks' worth of equipment and materials until you've tried it. Who knows, it may not be your cup of tea. You may find yourself frustrated and clumsy at the fine handwork that it takes, or maybe your eyes aren't good enough for that fine detail. We find ourselves thinking of all the things we could be doing instead—like fishing. Lots of guys say there's no better way to watch a football game, because you can actually do something constructive during those interminable time-outs and commercials, and you can look up from the vise when something actually happens. And by the way, women often make excellent fly tyers. Their fingers are usually smaller and more nimble, and many women have a nice, delicate touch that's hard for a guy to imitate.

If you're going to get set up to tie flies, you'll need a basic set of tools and some basic materials:

- Vise
- Bobbin
- Good scissors
- Hackle pliers
- Dubbing needle
- Head cement
- Hair stacker
- Marabou & chenille
- Pheasant & turkey tails
- Whip finisher

- Assorted hooks
- Threads and tinsels
- Peacock herl (peacock's tail feathers)
- Saddle hackle, brown & grizzly capes
- Muskrat, hare & assorted dubbings
- Various yarns
- Elk, moose & deer hair hide patches
- Good table with bright top
- Good light (very important!)

Parts of the Fly

To understand how to tie flies, we first need to understand the parts of a hook. Starting from the front of the hook, the eye is what allows us to tie the hook to a line. Going back, the shank of the hook is what holds the materials that

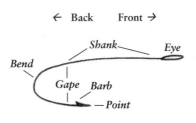

make up a fly. The bend in the hook is self-explanatory; it leads to the point, which is the sharp part. The barb, of course, extends downward from the point. The distance between the point and the shank is the "gape," or gap, depending on who is defining the terms.

The parts of a dry fly are distinctly different from the hook. The head of the fly is right behind the eye—it's typically a wrapping of thread. The hackle is the series of extended fibers that radiate all the way around the hook, directly behind the eye. The wings are the twin extensions, usually tiny feathers, immediately behind the hackle. The wing and hackle together are called the

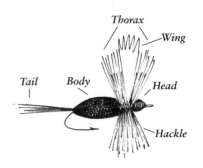

thorax, which corresponds to that part of the actual insect. Behind the thorax we have the body of the fly, which is usually dubbing and/or tinsel wrappings. The tail is often made of three or four strands of elk or deer hair.

A nymph is similar to a dry fly, except that a nymph almost never has wings, but does sometimes have legs that extend below the thorax, and ribbing wrapped around the body of the fly. Some patterns call for a wing case to be tied around the thorax.

The Adam's Example

For every fly there is a "recipe," or a standard set of instructions. It will specify which size and type of hook, which materials to use, and how to affix them to the hook. Typically, each fly takes about six steps to create. In this case, we're going to show you how to tie an Adam's Special, which is a very typical dry mayfly pattern.

1. *Wrapping:* The process begins with wrapping the body of the hook with thread.

2. *Tail:* Then, the tail is attached. Leave enough material to extend most of the length of the hook, then wrap it with thread to bind it to the hook.

3. *Body:* Now it's time to make the body of the fly, as specified in the recipe. Many bodies are created from dubbings, which are simply a fine woolly material rubbed onto a strand of thread. In our case the dubbing is muskrat hair, which has been run through a coffee grinder. First we coat the thread with a little wax to catch the dubbing. Then we pull a dab of dubbing from the pouch, rub it onto the thread until we have a fat thread about four inches long, then wrap it onto the hook. It's important that your dubbing doesn't

get too thick, or the body of the fly will have a bulging appearance.

4. *Wings:* Pull a couple of thin feathers from the grizzly hackle (which is the cape from a gray rooster's neck) and wrap them around the hook until they're just the height you want. Bind them to the hook with thread.

5. *Hackle:* The hackle is what makes the fly float. It is created by wrapping a feather from a brown rooster's cape around the head of the hook so that the individual filaments of the feather are separated from one another, providing buoyancy on the water.

6. *Whip Finish:* The loose end of the thread must be tightly wrapped around the head of the hook. The "whip finisher" is the tool needed to tie this knot.

6. *Cement:* Once the hackle is wrapped and affixed with thread, it's very important to cement the head of the hook. If you neglect to cement the head, it's very likely that your flies will unravel while fishing, much to your chagrin and embarrassment. However, be careful with the stuff. Many is the time that you'll dose a fly too liberally with cement and actually close the eye of the hook. It's no big deal unless you're standing in the middle of the river at dusk with fish rising all around you, and you're trying to poke your tippet through the eye of a hook that's been cemented shut.

Getting Started

Tying a nymph such as a Hare's Ear is very similar to this dry fly pattern, except that there are no wings. On some nymphs, the recipe calls for a wing casing in the thorax area, which involves wrapping in a body of material such as a grouse feather or a bit of turkey tail.

Some recommended patterns for a beginning tyer include nymphs such as the Hare's Ear, Prince Nymph, Brown Hackle Peacock, and Pheasant Tail; streamers such as the Woolly Bugger and Woolly Worm; and dry flies such as the Elk Hair Caddis, Adams Special, Light Cahill and Royal Wulff.

If you're really interested in tying, we recommend that you start by learning a dozen or two dozen patterns and perfecting them. Once you get good at those patterns, then you might think about experimenting with your own creations. As with any new endeavor, you'll be far ahead of the game by taking classes. If you try to learn it on your own, you'll re-invent the wheel several times and risk becoming totally frustrated. There are many good books on fly tying, but they're a lot like cookbooks—pretty boring stuff if you're looking for lively reading. (Note: We recommend reading Gary Borger's books on fly tying if you are interested in getting started.)

Be careful with fly tying. You might get addicted, and you'll find yourself wondering if the dog would mind if you shaved just a little patch of hair off his rump so you can try that new pattern you just invented. Or, maybe you'll find yourself walking down the highway with a shovel and a plastic bag, furtively scooping up an interesting dead bird for thorax material. At the very least, you can spend many hundreds of dollars on new and exotic materials, and your mate might threaten divorce if you don't leave the tying bench to go out for dinner once in a while.

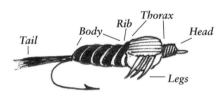

How The "H&L Variant" Got Its Name

by Gary Hubbell

One of the wonderful things about flyfishing is the naming of the flies we use. There is no rhyme or reason to it, other than the fancy of the tyer who devised the fly. Actually, you can tell a lot about the man or woman who thought up a new pattern simply by the way it is named. Some tyers are poetic, others lyrical, others analytical, while a few are simply boring. Fly names like the "Irresistible," the "Royal Coachman," and the "Pink Lady" are some of the colorful names that enrich an angler's fly box. Interestingly enough, the most colorful names seem to belong to dry fly attractor patterns.

Then there are the more staid and serious "bread and butter" patterns that see a lot of everyday use, like the "Brown Hackle Peacock," the "Hare's Ear," and the "Elk Hair Caddis," which are patterns that reflect quite literally which materials are used to tie them.

Some tyers become very analytical with their creations, calling them after the Latin names of the insects they imitate, and even the transitory stage of the insect. That's why we have "Choronomid" midge patterns and "Baetis Emergers."

The most interesting fly name I know of, however, was coined by a President in a spontaneous moment. In the 1950's, it was well known to the American public that President Dwight D. Eisenhower loved to fish. Eisenhower had a friend by the name of Aksel Nielsen, who owned a large ranch on St. Louis Creek near Fraser, Colorado. It was fair enough fishing, but it became great fishing when Eisenhower announced his plans to join Nielsen for a fishing retreat. The Colorado fish and game boys promptly drove up to Nielsen's creek and dumped in a horde of 4- to 5-pound rainbows in anticipation of Ike's visit.

Aksel wanted to make sure that Ike had a good time, so he called up his old friend Ralph Coffman, a Denver schoolteacher who moonlighted tying flies for sporting goods stores. Coffman tied up a selection of flies for Ike's trip, including a black-and-white concoction that Coffman had generically named the "All-Purpose Variant." The AP Variant was sort of a bastardized fly. Its origins came from the Red Quill, a popular pattern among Western anglers of the day. Coffman knew of the Red Quill's effectiveness from fishing his favorite river, the Frying Pan, where he was struggling to make the payments on a small fishing house on the riverbank. Those who know the lower Pan can tell you that there's a lot of rough, broken water, and the Red Quill didn't ride the whitewater very well. It got waterlogged. Also, it presented problems of visibility, because the red sandstone bottom of the Frying Pan blended so easily with the colors of the Red Quill.

So Coffman took the basic pattern of the fly and changed it around. He replaced the feathery wings of the Red Quill with bristly white impala hair, and changed the tail to the same material. Then he changed the body of the fly from a dusty red color to a black peacock herl. When he was finished, the dimensions were basically the same as the Red Quill, but it was an altogether different fly. It was a black and white attractor pattern similar to a Royal Wulff.

When Eisenhower got to Colorado, he found that his vision had been failing him and he needed a visible fly. The hatchery trout had devoured most of the available insects in St. Louis Creek, and they were hungry. Ralph Coffman's black and white AP Variant must have looked mighty good to them, because they ate it up. The President caught lots of fish. Of course, the White House press corps had accompanied Ike to Colorado, but for the most part they were barred from traipsing down to the creek with him. When he got back from fishing, they were hungry for any scrap of news. One of the reporters shouted, "Mr. President! What's your favorite fly?"

"Why, this one," Ike said, holding up the AP Variant. "That fly caught everything, including the house and lot." The name stuck. The fly promptly became the House and Lot, or the H&L Variant. It's actually a very fitting name, because that's what it bought for

Ralph Coffman. Once the national media seized on the story of the wonder fly, Coffman was buried with orders. In just one spring, Coffman and his wife, Eleanor, tied 400 dozen of the House and Lot alone. The proceeds from the fly business paid off a nice little fishing place on the Frying Pan—both the house and the lot.

Chapter Eleven
Equipment

*F*lyfishing is like anything—you can spend too much money or too little. You can go down to the variety store and buy a "complete flyfishing combo!" for under a hundred bucks, and a month later you'll find yourself regretting the decision. Or, you can walk into a full-retail fly shop during high season and spend a couple thousand bucks if you aren't careful. There is a happy medium. The best way to find out what you want in fishing gear is to fish with a few friends, try their equipment and see what their perceptions are. Cast several rods. Check out their vests, ask them what they think you need and what you don't need. Be careful, though. Flyfishing can be a real gadget sport, with all kinds of special glasses, thermometers, fly boxes, nets, flashlights, raingear—the list is endless. All you really need is a fly rod, a reel, a line, a leader, a net, some strike indicators, weight, tippet, forceps and a few flies.

Rods

This is your most important acquisition. First, however, you need to know what you're looking for. Rods are categorized by weight—that is, as we've already explained, the fly line must have weight in order to throw it. Exactly how much the fly line weighs, and the rod it matches, determines the weight of the rod. The smaller the number, the lighter the rod. On the extreme ends of the spectrum, a 1-weight rod is very, very light, used for very small trout or panfish in very small streams (there is even a "0" weight rod available now); a 12-weight rod is extremely heavy, intended for catching deep-sea fish weighing hundreds of pounds.

A 5-weight or 6-weight rod is a very typical fly rod used for medium to large trout streams and rivers. A 7-weight rod is used for big, wide rivers where long casts and big fish are the rule. A 3-weight rod would be a good choice for smaller trout on a spring creek, where delicate casts and fine line control are necessary.

Length is also an important consideration. One summer Jerry Siem, chief rod designer for Sage Rod Company, showed us a 5½ -foot 3-weight rod for very tight brushy creeks, but that's an extremely short rod. Some fishermen like to use a 10-foot or even longer rod for nymph fishing or for long casts on big rivers, but a normal rod is 8½ or 9 feet. Gary uses an 8½-foot rod for the simple reason that when he breaks it down and puts it in the rod tube, it fits behind the seat of his truck. A nine-footer is too long. John, like most Western anglers, uses a 9-foot rod.

Then there is the question of action. Rods are given the classification of slow, medium, medium-fast, or fast action. English rods are rather like English Labrador retrievers—slow and methodical. American rods tend to be fast. We asked John Bailey, owner of Dan Bailey's Fly Shop in Livingston, Montana, his thoughts about rod selection, and his reply was, "Well, it has a lot to do with how people fish. If they want to stand in one hole and fish it for two hours, they'll probably be happy with a slow action. If they can't stand still and they cover half a mile of river in those two hours, they'll want a fast action."

This may be hard to understand just from reading words on a page, but you'll see what we mean when you cast a fast and a slow rod. With a fast action, the tip responds quickly to the fisherman's muscles. When the wrist snaps forward to finish a cast, the rod responds instantly and throws the line forward. After the cast is complete, the tip vibrates momentarily and stops. A slow action requires more patience and a slower pace in casting. If you're not used to a slow action, you must stop and think "Pause!" at each stroke. At the end of a stroke, the tip may vibrate for a couple of seconds.

Each has its advantages and disadvantages. Because the tip on a slow-action rod is so soft, it's easy to mend the line and correct a drift. But a faster rod has the power to throw a fly a long way, with a tight loop, and very accurately. However, the faster rod can also mean a stiff tip that can cause more fish to break off on the hook set. Many old-timers prefer the slower actions because they are similar to the bamboo rods that they learned on.

For the beginning fisherman, we recommend a 5-weight or 6-weight rod, 8½ to 9 feet in length, medium to medium-fast action. A fast action might frustrate a beginner because it requires an expert's touch, but a slow action is sometimes just too slow. If you know you'll be fishing a particular stretch of water very often, such as a small stream or a big wide river, you might want to go lighter or heavier in weight, but a 5- or 6-weight rod is an ideal choice.

Most rods come as two-piece rods joined by a ferrule that slips together in the middle. Materials are various; over time, rods have evolved from bamboo to steel to fiberglass to graphite and boron and several other space-age materials. We don't recommend a fiberglass rod. If you've got one in the garage from Grandpa, give yourself a break and get a decent graphite rod. A good-quality graphite rod can be had for as little as $200, and a very nice rod can be found for $300-500. Avoid cheap junk, or you'll just be buying a decent rod a month or two down the road when you get frustrated with your cheap one.

Just so you know what makes a rod cheap or expensive, look closely at the components of the rod. Is the grip made from good, clean cork or is it knotty? Are the guides wrapped tightly and professionally, or are the wrappings sloppy and bulging with glue? Is the rod sanded and gleaming, or is the blank rough and unfinished (this is often a major cost-saver for rod companies' cheaper models). Is the reel seat machined of good aluminum, or is it cast of cheap material? Is it an "uplocking" reel seat (the reel fits snugly under the cork grip) or is it a sloppy set of double locking rings? Is the reel seat rosewood or some other exotic hardwood, or is it plastic and cast aluminum?

Over time, you'll figure out what kind of rod you like, and you'll know what to look for when you're buying a new rod. Like the serious shotgun shooter who has a gun cabinet full of double-barrels ranging from .410 to 12-gauge, it's easy to fall into collecting fly rods until there are six or seven stowed in the new fly-tying room. When you're at that point, you might think about building your own rod, which entails buying a blank from a known manufacturer and wrapping the guides, assembling the handle, and finishing the rod yourself, complete with signature.

Pack rods deserve mention also, because they fill a nice niche in fishing. I know several businessmen who toss a pack rod, a reel, and a few flies in with their luggage when they go on business trips, because you just never know when you might find good fishing. They're great for backpacking trips, motorcycle sojourns, horse pack trips—any time when the rod should be compact. The combinations are various, from 3-piece to as many as 8-piece rods. Four-piece pack rods are typical. Just be advised that for each new joint in a rod, a little bit of action is compromised. However, these rods are getting better with new technology. It's a real art to build a good pack rod. Some pack rods feel like they're "hinged" when you cast them, as if the rod casts in stages that relate to the breaks in the rod. For a serious fisherman, however, a good pack rod is a necessary acquisition.

Reels

Now comes the question of reels. Once a fishing client asked us, "So what is the difference between a cheap reel and an expensive one? They all do the same thing, don't they?"

Our reply was, "Yes, but so do wristwatches. What's the difference between a Timex and a Rolex? They both tell time, don't they?" Funny, too that the price range is so similar, from $40 for an old faithful Pflueger Medalist to $2,500 for a fancy gold-plated reel.

A reel is really a very simple mechanism whose function is to store line when you don't need it, and let it out when you do need it. They have a drag, usually adjustable, that controls how much force is exerted before it lets out line. When you've got a big fish on, you want him to be able to pull line out of the reel so he doesn't snap the line. Less expensive reels usually have a "pawl" drag, or a system utilizing a couple of clickers and a spring. They work fine, but they're usually loud. More expensive reels use a disc drag much like disc brakes on a car. The best ones are made of machined metal, though it's not uncommon to see plastic disc reels.

The biggest differences among reels, however, are intangibles like their look and feel. We personally don't like a reel that has a really loud drag. When a fisherman is stripping line out of a loud reel on a quiet stream, it sounds very unnatural. Action is important, too. You can just feel a smooth action, and that also makes it easy to fight a fish.

Reels are made to hold certain weights of line, usually in groups of three. The smallest reels hold line weights 1, 2, and 3, medium reels hold weights 4,5, and 6, and large reels hold weights 7, 8, and 9. Freshwater reels are cheaper than saltwater reels because it's not so important to build corrosion-resistant parts. Saltwater reels for heavy lines and big fish can get very, very expensive—$500 or more for a decent reel. A good trout reel for line weights 4, 5, and 6 can be found for $70-$120. Look for a reel that has a nice smooth feel, good machined metal parts, and a quiet adjustable drag.

One last note about reels: almost all of them are adjustable so you can reel from the left side. We think it's crazy to fish all day with the rod in your right hand, and precisely at the moment when you hook a fish, switch the rod over to the unfamiliar left hand just so you can crank a reel with the right hand. We switch all our reels over to reel from the left, and usually there's a diagram in a new reel box to show you how to do it. Normally it's a simple matter of loosening one or two screws, flipping the direction of a couple of "pawls" and tightening the screws again.

Now, remember that if you have several different weight rods, you're going to need different lines. You can either buy new reels and put new lines on all of them, or have a couple of trusty reels for which you have extra spools loaded with different lines.

Lines

You've come this far, now don't skimp on the line. If you're going to spend money, spend it on your fly line. A cheap line will cast poorly, float poorly, and break down quickly. Spend some money for a good line. Again, there are all kinds of fly lines, from sinking tips for deep nymphing to saltwater casting lines. John prefers a floating "weight-forward" line, where most of the weight is loaded in the first few feet of the line. This type of line casts more easily in windy conditions.

For a good all-around line, we prefer a double-tapered floating fly line that matches your rod in weight. The term "double tapered" refers to the construction of the line, which is thinner at each end and comes to a gradual thickest point at the middle. This is also handy when the line starts to wear out, because you can take it off the reel and put the worn end back on the reel first. Because the second half of the line is rarely used, you basically have a new line. Be careful not to mismatch rod and line. A 5-weight rod will do a miserable job of throwing a 3-weight line because the line is too light. However, sometimes you'll have a rod matched with the correct weight line, but together they don't perform well. If you load it with a line that's one weight heavier than suggested, the performance may increase significantly.

Before you tie a line onto your reel, don't forget to put backing on the reel first. "Backing" is a term for a thin strong string wound around the spool that serves a dual purpose. The primary purpose is to serve as your ace in the hole should you ever get a really big fish on that strips your whole fly line out of your reel. If the fly line was all you had, you'd break off the fish when the drag stopped giving out line. But if you have backing tied to the fly line, that fish can keep pulling out line without breaking off. The other reason for using backing is to fill up the inside of the reel spool so that the fly line is closer to the outer rim of the reel. In that position, it's easier to take out line and reel it up. Backing is very cheap, and most fly shops or sporting goods stores will put it on your reel for a minimal cost when you buy the reel.

Fly lines wear out after a season or two if you use them a lot, but you can extend their lives by cleaning them periodically with soap and water. You know you're due for a new line when your old one is cracked and dirty-looking, and when it's hard to cast. Remember, when starting out it is best to have a fly shop professional help you set up your line properly.

Leaders

Leaders are one item that you'll use often. It's good to have three or four of them in your vest at all times. Flyfishing leaders are tapered, from a fat thick line that's approximately the diameter of a fly line, to a thin line next to the fly. Leaders are rated by diameter (i.e., strength) and length. The bigger the number, the finer the leader, and of course, they have different purposes. For example, a 12-foot 7X leader is a long, very fine leader for fishing small flies to fish in slow, clear water. In water that has even a little bit of turbidity, a 5X leader is fine enough that fish won't see your line, and a 9-foot leader is a nice average length. If you're fishing for 6-pound brown trout in murky water, a heavy leader like a 2X might be the ticket. Overall, a standard leader is a 9-foot 4X or 9-foot 5X.

Just recently tackle manufacturers have come out with new "limp" leaders and other kinds of leaders for various situations, and, of course, they're very expensive. The good fishermen we know just use a standard leader and go right on catching fish. You'll find that certain cheap brands that you find at discount stores and hardware stores perform very poorly. Go to a good fly shop to buy your leaders.

Vests and Fanny Packs

Every fisherman needs a place to put things, and that's how the fishing vest evolved. As we said before, fishing can be a gadget sport, and the vest is what carries all the gadgets around. Look for a vest whose pockets will easily accommodate your fly boxes; that fits loosely and comfortably; that has a D-ring to hang a net; a back pocket to hold a raincoat and a water bottle; and is of good construction and materials.

Because some people hate having weight hanging around their necks, a trend has emerged to pack everything into a fanny pack. There are lots of good ones on the market, and they hold just about everything that a vest does. Look for packs that won't soak all your flies if you happen to get waist-deep in the water.

Each vest or fanny pack should have some equipment (notice we didn't say the entire fishing catalogue!) We suggest the following items:

- Clippers with retractable drawstring
- 2 fly boxes
- 3 dozen flies, assorted patterns
- Split shot or Twist-on lead weight
- 3 extra leaders (9-foot 4x)
- Strike indicators
- 4 spools of tippet (3x, 4x, 5x and 6x)
- net
- Forceps (preferably flat-bladed, with no serrations)
- Polarizing sunglasses
- Sunscreen

Don't go overboard on loading up your vest with gadgets. These are the basics that you'll need, and if you find through experience that you're lacking something, buy it later. Remember, if it's in your vest, you have to carry it around, and carrying 25 pounds in your vest is no fun. It's often the case that we guide fellows who show up with gadgets and equipment that we've never seen before. It's rarely the case that a gadget helps someone catch more fish.

Nets

Some fishermen prefer to fish without a net, but we like having one. There's a raging debate in flyfishing circles of whether it's better to release a fish with or without a net, and we've found that for beginners, using a net tends to quickly subdue a struggling fish so that we can get him back in the water faster. Others say nets damage fish, either from stripping their slime or from bending them double. If you're going to use a net, get one that's made either of soft cotton or of a fine mesh nylon.

Waders

As far as comfort is concerned, this is probably your most important acquisition. When the weather is cloudy and the water is cold, nothing beats a good pair of neoprene chest waders. Neoprene is the same material that divers and surfers use for wetsuits, except in this case it is meant to keep all the water out. This is one of those things where you get what you pay for.

It's possible to find decent neoprene chest waders for around $100, but we'd rather pay $225 and get a really good pair. The more expensive waders last longer, leak less, and are usually more comfortable.

Neoprene waders come in heavyweight (5 mm.) and lightweight (3 mm.) versions. The thicker waders are warmer, and generally more durable. One of the pitfalls to neoprene waders is that they're fairly easily punctured, which can be a drag. There are potions available to glue holes shut, and it's a good idea to buy some. You'll sweat inside your waders, which will leave them feeling damp and clammy. When you're done fishing, turn the waders inside out and hang them where there is good air circulation. Don't, however, hang them in the sun for long periods, because the sunlight will deteriorate the fabric. If you're storing them for long periods, make sure both the inside and outside of the fabric is clean and dry.

Another type of waders is the old canvas britches that Granddad wore. Do yourself a favor: leave these in the attic. Not only do they get brittle and leak a lot, they're heavy and dangerous. Because the canvas waders don't cling to your body like the neoprenes, if you fall in the river they will fill up with a lot of water, and that makes escaping from a swift current very difficult.

In the past few years, a couple of companies have come out with Gore-Tex waders, which are lightweight and comfortable, but still have some of the disadvantages of the old canvas waders. If you fall in, they'll fill up with water. However, for hot summer days these thin waders are just the ticket. The Gore-Tex helps your perspiration evaporate, and the thin material helps keep you cool. Wear a wading belt to minimize the amount of water that can flood into your waders should you fall.

Hip boots, made of rubber, Gore-Tex or neoprene, are fine for small streams and marshy bottoms, but you can easily get in water deeper than your hip boots, so be careful. If you're flying out to some unknown place to go fishing, chances are your hip boots won't be adequate. We go in deeper than hip-deep practically every time we go fishing.

If you buy stocking-foot chest waders, you'll need a pair of wading shoes. Again, you get what you pay for. Get a stout pair of good imitation-leather felt-soled shoes, and pay what they ask, which will likely be $90-150. Cheap ones go south on you quickly. We don't recommend leather shoes, unless you're patient enough to keep greasing them to keep them from shriveling up. Good felt soles are important because of their grip on slippery river bottoms.

And on those brilliant warm August days, why use waders at all? That's what we call "blue-legging it" in Colorado. As a matter of fact, Gary didn't own a pair of waders of any kind until he was 22 years old. It can be quite pleasant to stand in a cool river on a hot August day.

Times Have Changed

by Gary Hubbell

Though I'm only 36 years old, I feel as if I've experienced two different centuries of flyfishing. Flyfishing equipment has evolved so rapidly since I first picked up a fly rod that it feels like the difference between driving a Model T Ford and a new Porsche.

In *"A River Runs Through It,"* John and the producers were careful to depict the anglers in the movie as they looked when they were fishing in the 1920's—split bamboo rods, wicker creels, fedoras and chino pants. They didn't use vests, waders, graphite rods or alloy reels. Their lines were silk, leaders were catgut, hooks were snelled, and flies were kept in a small book that fit in a shirt pocket.

Though fishing equipment was beginning to evolve rapidly when I started fishing in the early 1970's, my father was not exactly at the forefront of the equipment revolution. In fact, we were very content fishing much like the Maclean family was depicted. My father had an old Wright & McGill Eagle Claw fiberglass rod with a Perrine automatic reel. He used a wicker creel or simply stuffed trout into the pockets of his fishing jacket. We had no waders. We simply waded into the snowmelt of the Roaring Fork and fished until we got too cold to cast anymore. We happily used the flies we bought at Kenny's Pharmacy with their thick snelled leaders.

We didn't really know the difference between "dry flies" and "nymphs." We rarely flyfished during the day, preferring to leave the house when the sun was setting over the ridge and fish until black dark. And by God, we caught fish.

Nowadays, if you were to show up at an access point and begin to fish using the equipment that we knew and loved, people would laugh you off the river. It would be like showing up at a ski area with leather boots and wooden skis (which I also learned to ski on).

Now I've got four or five different graphite rods in various weights and speeds; I've got machined alloy reels with space-age floating lines; I've got a vest filled with hundreds of different dry flies, emergers, nymphs and terrestrials. I've got waders in three different weights for different weather conditions, and I've got tippets as thin as a spider web. No doubt about it, nice equipment is fun to have, but I know one thing for sure: twenty years ago I had just as much fun with an old fiberglass rod, a silk line, a catgut leader and a half-dozen flies tied on snelled hooks.

Chapter Twelve
Knots, Leaders & Tippet

Knots are a very important part of flyfishing, because a knot can make the difference between success and failure. Nothing is quite so frustrating as losing a nice trout because your knot failed. There are people who get a warm fuzzy feeling when they talk about knots, and they can go on and on with endless variations of fishing knots.

We see knots in a more practical sense. We feel a fisherman can do practically anything he needs to do with just four knots, so we're going to teach you those four. There are really only two reasons for a flyfisherman to tie a knot: either to tie two different lines together, or to tie on a fly. In the process of rigging up, you'll only need three knots. But before you even tie a knot, there are some decisions that must be made:

1) How long a leader do I need?
2) What size tippet should I use?
3) What size fly should I use?

As we explained in "Chapter Four—Nymphing," there are several factors in determining how long a leader to use. At the minimum, a seven-foot leader is a good choice for tight situations like small, brushy streams. At the most, a 15-foot leader would be used for very deep rivers or lakes, or perhaps for a very still stream with extremely selective fish. We typically use a nine-foot leader, and that's a good all-around choice for most rivers and streams. Leaders are numbered by the diameter of the leader at the thin end, and they should be selected just like tippet.

There are a couple of variables for selecting tippet. Tippet is numbered as such: the smaller the number, the thicker the tippet, rather like shotgun pellets. 0X is a very heavy, thick, strong tippet for situations like salmon or ocean fishing. 3X is a sturdy, fairly heavy tippet used for trout fishing, and 5X is a fairly thin tippet commonly used for trout fishing. Some situations demand a very light, barely visible tippet, like 7X, and the thinnest tippet (like spider web) is 8X. For beginning fishermen, we recommend using 4x or 5x tippet in most situations. The tippet is strong enough to withstand some tugs if you get stuck on something, and still thin enough so that it won't deter a fish from striking.

Other factors in determining tippet selection include the turbidity of the water, the speed and strength of the current and the size of the fly. If you're fishing a big, fast, murky river with big flies and big fish, 3X tippet would be a good choice. If the stream is clear and slow, the flies small, and the fish very selective, 6X or 7X tippet would be a better choice. Some people say that if you divide the size of the fly by a factor of three, that should be the size of the tippet you should use. For example, a size 18 fly should be fished with 6X tippet, a size 12 with 4X, etc. But as we can both attest, we violate these rules with regularity and with great success. Don't get caught up in thinking that you're not catching fish because you're fishing with a tippet that's too heavy. We've fished size 20 flies on 4X tippet to big, strong fish, and we don't find much difference in how many strikes we get. It's much more a matter of presentation and line control than tippet size.

We hear stories all the time from guys who are very proud of fishing a very light tippet to big fish. That may be something for the experts to try (actually, we call them "tippet geeks,") but for beginners, don't try anything lighter than 5X, and there won't be as many fish swimming around with flies broken off in their mouths.

Nail Knot

After reading "Chapter Nine—Fly Selection," you should have a good idea of what size and pattern of fly that you want to cast, so now it's time to learn to rig up your line and tie on a fly. The first knot is the one that we use to tie the leader onto the fly line. It's

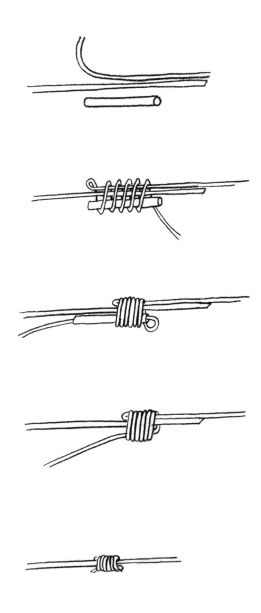

The Nail Knot—may be tied with or without nail

called the "nail knot," and it's usually illustrated on the packages that the leaders come in. This is probably the trickiest knot, but it's the one you use the least, because you don't need to change leaders that often. Many fly shops like to rig you up with a butt section— a stout two-foot piece of monofilament that acts as an intermediary between the leader and fly line. Lots of guys get lazy and use a simple loop knot to tie on new leaders to their butt section, but this has several inherent problems. First, it creates a hinged action when casting the leader. It lays down poorly, and it's hard to cast through the guides. Also, there's a big knot there that has a habit of catching on the end rod guide when you're trying to net a fish. It gives a struggling fish the perfect amount of tension to snap off the tippet. If you're going to use a butt section, you have to tie a good nail knot from the leader to the butt section. If you have trouble with it, take your leader into a fly shop and the guy behind the counter will give you a quick lesson and tie one for you.

First, to tie a nail knot, you match up the end of the fly line and the thick end of the leader so that they overlap about five inches. Then, take the end of the leader and wrap it around the fly line four times in a series of tight concentric loops. Make sure to hold these loops in sequence between your thumb and forefinger. Then, push the end of the leader through the four little loops that you've just created. Making sure to keep these loops in their proper order, slowly tighten each end of the leader coming out of the knot. The fly line stays in a passive position. Once the loops are tightened, the knot should be drawn tight from both ends, and it helps to nudge the loops of the knot together with your fingernails. When it's finished, the knot should look something like the barrel of a noose drawn around the fly line.

The nail knot is important because it is a very strong knot, and in the all-important joining of the fly line with the leader, strength is required. It must also be a low-profile knot, because it will often be the case that the knot is drawn through the end guide of the rod. If the knot is bulky, the line will catch on that rod tip, and bad things will happen, like a fish will suddenly have something solid to resist against and he'll break your line, or you won't be able to cast your fly line out again without having to stop and manually pull the line through the guides.

You'll notice that there is no "nail" in our "nail knot." Our knot is technically called an "on the water" nail knot because it's simpler and faster to tie. Most other guide books and knot illustrations show a nail being used as a pattern to wrap the leader around the fly line. Over time, we've found that the nail is just one more thing to hold onto and get in the way. Try it this way, and with a little practice, you'll get proficient at it.

Surgeon's Knot

The surgeon's knot is used to tie two pieces of tippet and/or a piece of tippet and the leader together. The function of the surgeon's knot is to join two similar pieces of material to make a single continuous line. A likely scenario might come about when you lose a fly on a bush, and you need to tie on a new piece of 5X tippet to your old 3X leader. The surgeon's knot is very, very simple. Simply overlap the two pieces of tippet about five inches. Make a loop of both pieces of tippet. Then thread the long end through the loop twice. Thread the short end through the loop twice. Gently draw the knot tight. That's it. If you like, you can draw each end through the loop three times for a stronger knot. The knot is so simple that some people suspect it of weakness. That's not the case. The surgeon's knot is a strong, dependable knot, and if you wrap the long ends and short ends together, tensile strength is increased.

The surgeon's knot is the simplest knot to join two pieces of tippet, so you might think it's not as strong as other more complicated knots, like the blood knot. Not true, according to Bob Wynn, one of our guiding clients. Bob is a retired engineer who has nothing better to do than sit around testing the breaking point of different knots with a spring tension measuring device. He says the surgeon's knot is the strongest, and we'll take his word for it.

The Blood Knot

There's another good knot that's used to tie two pieces of tippet together, and that's called the blood knot. The blood knot is tougher to tie than the surgeon's knot, but it looks more polished and might slip through your rod guides a little easier. It works like this: take

Double Surgeon's
(may be drawn tight)

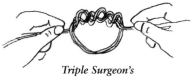

Triple Surgeon's

The Surgeon's Knot

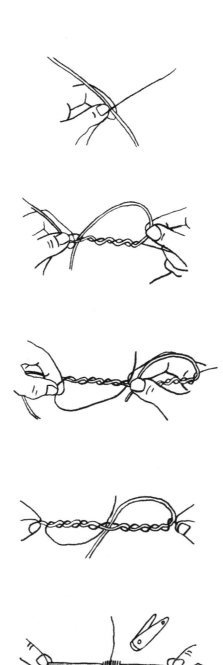

The Blood Knot

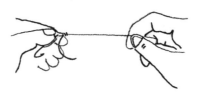

The Improved Clinch Knot

156

the two lines you want to tie together and cross them to form an X by pinching them together between your thumb and forefinger of your right hand. Take the tail protruding from the left side and wrap it four to five times around the main line directly below it. Then take the tail you've just wrapped and place it at the right side of the V you're holding with your thumb and forefinger. Pinch it off with your left thumb and forefinger. Now wrap the protruding right tail four to five times around the main line directly below it. Take that tail and thread it through the old V, which is now a loop in the middle of the knot, pointing the opposite direction of the other tail. Then draw the knot tight on both sides. Note that wrapping the right tail in the opposite direction of the left tail determines the success of this knot.

The Improved Clinch Knot

So, now we've learned how to tie a leader to a fly line and how to tie two tippets together, so it's time to learn how to tie on a fly. This is the knot you will use the most. It's called the improved clinch knot, also known as the fisherman's knot, and you just learned how to tie it by learning the blood knot. Push the end of the tippet through your fly and overlap it about two inches. Wrap the short end around the tippet five or six times. Push the short end back through the eyelet created by wrapping the line around itself. At this point, you have what's called a clinch knot, and it's an effective knot, but we like to go one step further. Take the short end and push it through the big loop created by pushing the short end through the eyelet. Carefully draw the knot tight, and clip the short end off close.

General Advice

Some words to the wise about knots: it is very important that your knots be drawn tight. A loose knot will fail. But in the process of drawing a knot tight, it's important not to draw it too tight. You see, monofilament is funny stuff. You can actually cut through monofilament with itself. If you lubricate the knot a little (a smidgen of spit does just fine), your chances are better of having a nice, tight knot without cutting itself. Clip the loose ends of your knots closely, but not so close that the knot will slip loose. We like to leave about a millimeter of tippet ends. Don't use a knife to cut loose ends—use fingernail clippers or fisherman's clips. Remember that the knot looks different underwater than it does in the air. A long loose end on a clinch knot will often hold a big bubble of air around it when it's fished underwater, making your fly look completely unnatural.

Check your knots by giving a firm tug when you think you're finished. Sometimes they'll slip loose, to your surprise. It's better to test it, break it, and start over than to lose a nice trout because you tied a sloppy knot. Also, check your tippet for fraying and wind knots. (Wind knots occur when the leader unknowingly catches on itself during a cast; knots will suddenly appear.) If you've managed to form a "wind knot" in your tippet, it's a firm guarantee that your line will break right there when you get a nice fish on. You should periodically check your line for wind knots and simply break off the line and tie a surgeon's or blood knot in its place.

Try to match your tippet with your leader. Sometimes tippet made by one manufacturer won't join well with a leader or tippet made by another manufacturer, so find one kind you like and stick with it. Be very careful when using mosquito repellent and later touching your fly line. If the repellent contains DEET, it will melt right through a monofilament line, even in minute quantities. If you've recently applied bug juice and then touch your leader or tippet, chances are good that the first fish you hook will snap your line. If you don't believe us, read the directions on a bottle of insect repellent. It will advise you to keep the stuff away from polyester clothes, watch crystals, and most plastics.

Knots don't have to be intimidating. The best way to learn them is to sit down and practice in front of the TV with string or heavy test monofilament at first. Knots are much more difficult if the light is failing, you're tired from wading the river all day, and your fingers are stiff and cold, so it's a good idea to practice before you go fishing. Knots can be a nice challenge, and there are dozens more that can be used for flyfishing—and if you learn just two or three more, you'll probably know more than most fishermen.

The Old Man's Knot

by John Dietsch

"Wanted: Men In Their Seventies. Must Be Excellent Fly Casters. Meet At Sacajawea Park Sunday, 10 A.M. Bring Flyfishing Equipment." This was how the advertisement read which I had placed in the local Livingston newspaper. I figure it was the first "casting" casting call in the history of film and television, but I could be wrong...

On Sunday morning about thirty Montana locals showed up: weathered faces, ribbed hands, wool shirts, hats from the attic, and fly lines cutting through the air. Robert Redford, the director of *"A River Runs Through It,"* was looking for the "Old Man" character who appears briefly at the beginning and end of the film. He was to play Norman Maclean in his seventies. One by one, I had the men sign in and walk toward the end of the dock by the pond in Sacajawea Park, near the Yellowstone River. Within just a few short seconds, I could tell whether or not the gentleman was a good caster or not.

Surprisingly, only six of the men had decent casts, and really only two of them had the "right look"—one of the men was quite a bit older than the other one and had deeply etched wrinkles, cool blue eyes, and thick tufts of white hair. However, he somehow looked too fragile to me. The younger man, in his late sixties, seemed to personify the Norman Maclean I had heard about—strong, opinionated, handsome, and direct. Having chosen these two men among the thirty, I dismissed everyone else and began casting with them, talking to them, and tying knots. The latter task would be asked of the character on camera in the film's final scene, so it was important to see how each of them carried it out.

The younger gentleman showed me how he tied his flies to the tippet with a clinch knot. He slid the tip of the monofilament into the eye of the hook with finesse, and smoothly wrapped the tag end around the line, just above the hook like a spiral. Then he adeptly brought the tag end through the opening in the line, just above the eye. He wet the line with his mouth and pulled tight. The whole process took under thirty seconds.

"There," the younger man said with a smile, "a clinch knot."

"Impressive," I replied.

The older man stood to my left, and although I was half expecting him to be watching the younger man—his competition—tie the clinch knot, I realized that he was concentrating on tying his own knot. I excused myself from the younger man, and walked over to the older gentleman.

"What are you tying?" I asked him.

He looked at me, with a sheepish grin, and said simply "My eyes aren't so good anymore."

His hands shook with the ferocity that only old age could induce. Between his poor eyesight and his trembling fingers, he had yet to simply thread the tippet through the eye of the hook, let alone tie the knot.

"Do you know how to tie a clinch knot?" I asked patiently. Again, the painful smile crept up on his mouth, and he shook his head slightly.

"No," he replied, pausing for a long moment.

A red light went off in my head. I thought, 'This guy can't even thread the line through the eye and he doesn't know what a clinch knot is.' Suddenly, I thought that the older man could never work as Norman on camera, but I kept the thought to myself.

"I tie a turle knot," he continued. "Do you know what a turle knot is?" he asked.

"I've heard of it," I replied, "but I don't know how to tie one." Then I thought 'perhaps you could show me how to tie it if you could just thread the damn line through the eye of the fly!'

It had been a good minute-plus, and still the old man had yet to thread the line through.

"There we go," he said with finality. "Takes me a bit longer than it used to. I'm sorry," he said, sensing my youthful impatience.

"No, that's quite alright," I said, not letting my true feelings show.

He proceeded to tie his turle knot, twisting the line so that it formed a loop that would slide back against the eye of the hook. I felt the clock ticking in my head, and imagined a camera rolling thousands of dollars' worth of film while this man's trembling hands attempted to tie this ancient knot.

"You know this is an old knot," he said to me, his hands shaking like the San Andreas fault. "Most everybody used this knot in the old days here in Montana...it takes a bit more time to tie than a clinch knot, but I think it's a better knot—worth the extra time."

I felt like saying, "Do you really know what time is worth here?" I could hardly contain the voices in my head—an impatience had developed in me from being around a film crew twenty-four hours a day, similar to someone who spends most of his day in traffic on the freeway. I don't recall ever letting the old man finish his turle knot. As I remember, I told him that there was no need for him to finish the knot (since it had been about five minutes)! So I never did learn how to tie it, but I did end up learning something about myself.

That afternoon, I presented Redford with the photographs of both men and explained that each of them had a beautiful cast. I then gave him my opinion that I felt the younger man might be a better choice since the older man would probably have a terrible time tying a knot on camera.

"Why's that?" the director asked astutely.

"Because his hands shake violently. He can hardly even thread the line through a hook!" I replied with exasperation.

Redford paused for a moment and looked at the picture of the older man again.

"Excellent," he answered. "I'd like to meet him tomorrow."

The older man, Arnold Richardson, had lived in Montana most of his life, and to play the part of Norman Maclean was both an honor and the memory of a lifetime. The shaking hands struggling to tie a knot at the end of the film are a trademark of the movie, and tell a story in themselves. Looking back at it, in my haste to "succeed," I had lost my sense of compassion while working on the film, and in so doing I had missed the magic that unfolded right in front of my eyes. I missed the message on the backs of the old man's veined, transparent, and leathered hands—the yearning that any man his age, feeling this passage of time, would have for younger days—the gentle acceptance that indeed those day were gone forever.

Chapter Thirteen

Boats

We have talked extensively about flyfishing while wading in this book, and that's how a beginner should learn: with both feet on the bottom of the riverbed. Taking a beginner into a boat to learn how to flyfish is like taking a beginning skier up to the black diamond runs to learn how to ski.

As you progress as a flyfisherman, however, you might find it an appealing prospect to learn to fish from a boat. You can have a grand old time floating down a river in a drift boat or raft, casting to fish after fish in pool after pool. But woe to the poor caster or inexperienced fisherman. It can be extremely frustrating if you don't know what you're doing. Think about it this way—how good a caster are you standing in the back yard on solid ground? Can you hit a coffee can from 30 feet away consistently? Maybe? Okay. Now try jogging along at five miles an hour with constantly changing targets, and see if you can hit that same coffee can 30 feet away. Fishing from a boat can be very challenging.

Drift Boats

Drift boats, or McKenzie river dories, as they are sometimes known, are the ultimate flyfishing craft. They're built with an upswept bow and stern, so they look like an upturned leaf sitting on the water. Drift boats are made of aluminum, fiberglass or wood, and they range from 14 to 18 feet in length. They can navigate fairly shallow rivers—they draft as little as four inches—and they're capable of handling up to Class IV whitewater.

However, drift boats can swamp and sink, so a river guide must know his craft very well. The occasional jagged rock protruding from the water or a series of nasty rapids can wreck a boat and dump the occupants in the river. A drift boat is, however, a superb flyfishing craft because two anglers can cast standing up with their legs supported by a special brace. Or, if they choose, the casters can be seated.

The caster in the front of the boat, or the bow, should cast to the pockets and seams next to the banks of the river. If the bow of the boat is 12 o'clock and he's casting to the left bank, the caster should cast to 11 o'clock and drift until his fly reaches 9 o'clock, or the midpoint of the boat. The caster in the stern may cast to the oarlocks, or middle, of the boat and drift all the way behind the boat. Each caster must be courteous enough to avoid hooking his fellow angler and the oarsman. If the angler in front is right-handed, he may cast normally, outside his body. If the angler in back is right-handed, he must false cast above his left shoulder to avoid hooking anybody with his cast.

It's the oarsman's job to keep the boat in an optimum casting position, and because the boat is typically flowing in a faster current than the anglers are fishing, he should backrow against the current to slow the boat for a better drift. The oarsman must be a well-trained, knowledgeable, talented individual. Not only must he know the river by heart, he must also be aware of the continually changing fishing conditions, and he should be a good instructor as well. Consequently, most good rowers are full-time guides, and a full-day float trip costs as much as $400.

Rigging up a rod for a float trip is different than rigging for a wading excursion. It's hard to spot a small fly from a drift boat, so anglers most often use big, bright flies. Hopper patterns are late-summer favorites. Most guides rig up at least two flies, and they often use much heavier tippet—such as 2x—than they would on a wade trip. One popular rig involves using a dry fly for the lead fly, six or seven feet down the leader, and a nymph and weight for a dropper. The nymph is rigged with three or four feet of tippet. That way, if there's a strike on the dry, it's easily visible, but if there's a strike on the nymph, the dry acts as a strike indicator.

During the late fall or early spring, when browns and rainbows are spawning, streamers can work wonders from a drift boat.

Effective fishing from a drift boat requires accurate casting and effective line control. No matter how good you are while wading, the first time you start casting from a dory you'll be overwhelmed. It all happens so fast. It usually takes at least a couple of hours for newcomers to get things sorted out, and that's if they're decent fishermen to start with. First-time flyfishermen are advised not to try it until they have some experience.

Releasing a fish from a drift boat is also quite a trick, and to do it right, sometimes you're better off pulling over to the bank to fight the fish and release it. We've had some pretty wild times trying to boat a fish while running Class III whitewater, and it's just easier on the trout if you can avoid handling them in the boat.

It takes a pretty big river to float a drift boat. The Roaring Fork, our home river, doesn't get big enough to float consistently until it joins with the Crystal River at Carbondale. Still, the Roaring Fork is one of the trickier rivers to float because of the changing currents and rocky bottom. The Colorado near Glenwood Springs is a great river to float, and it actually receives little pressure. Other rivers, such as the Green River below Flaming Gorge Reservoir in northeast Utah, see as many as 400 dories a day coursing down the river.

Montana has some great drift boat waters, such as the Madison and Yellowstone Rivers, the headwaters of the Missouri, and the Clark Fork River. The Bighorn is a classic drift boat river. Big, deep and wide, the Bighorn below Yellowtail Reservoir is one of the easiest rivers to float. The North Platte near Saratoga, Wyoming is a great river to float as well. Of course, the many salmon and steelhead rivers of the Northwest are easily fished by drift boats. There are good local guide services that float all these rivers, so if you want to book a trip, the Internet is a great place to look them up. However, be wary, because nothing can replace personal referrals.

If you want to get your own boat, grab your checkbook. They cost between $5,000 and $10,000 for new ones, although you can find decent used boats for around $2,500. We do not advise floating a river until you've had instruction from a competent, preferably licensed professional.

Float Tubes

The float tube is a simple device that hearkens back to summer days of sitting in an inner tube as a kid. Here's how it works: the manufacturer covers an O-shaped or U-shaped multi-chambered inflatable rubber bladder with a cloth shell, then stretches a seat between the side of the tube. The seat leaves a place for your legs to dangle underneath, which is your method of propulsion. The fisherman wears neoprene chest waders and scuba fins, which he laces over his fishing boots. It's a comical sight to watch somebody waddle into a lake wearing scuba fins and a big fat ring around his waist, but it's a great way to catch trout in lakes, ponds, and slow-moving rivers.

One of the disadvantages to a float tube is that the angler is suspended basically waist-deep in the water. That means your casting technique had better be fairly polished, because sloppy casting and float tubing do not go together. There is little margin for error because the angler is so low to the water. The advantage of float tubing is that it's quiet and peaceful, and fish don't notice you slipping in on them like they notice a boat.

Float tubing is not advised for waters where waves could swamp a fisherman, and it doesn't mix well with motorboats and Jet Skis. There's just too much danger that someone could swamp an angler with a wake or fail to see your low profile and run over you.

Typical methods of fishing from a float tube run the gamut, from stripping streamers to casting small dry flies. It's a perfect method of fishing a high-country lake or remote pond where no boats can go, and we've hooked up dozens of fish in a few hours from a float tube. It's very easy to release a trout from a float tube, too, because the trout are easily handled when they're right in front of you. However, float tubes are not advised for river fishing, because of the danger of getting tangled up in underwater obstructions.

Float tubes are a very safe method of fishing a lake, especially since they usually have multiple chambers that prevent the tube from collapsing if they become punctured at one point. However, it's a slow way of getting across a body of water. If the wind is picking up or a thunderstorm is rolling in, you can be very vulnerable to awful weather and even lightning. It's a good idea to keep an eye on your surroundings and be able to move off the water in five minutes or so.

Inflatable Boats

We used to fish out of inflatable rafts twenty years ago, but the new technology available makes our old rafts look obsolete. There are now inflatable pontoon boats with self-bailing features, anglers' chairs, and a high profile for easy casting. They're light and maneuverable, good whitewater boats, and great for reaching parts of the river where the channels are too narrow and shallow for a drift boat. They are not, however, as comfortable as a drift boat, and they won't accommodate as much gear or people. Usually it's a load to have one angler and one oarsman on many of the inflatable fishing boats.

On a smaller scale, some of the more inventive float tube manufacturers have combined the concept of pontoon boats and float tubes, making a smaller twin-hulled pontoon boat about five feet long. These are handy little fishing crafts. They hold one angler and his gear, and they have small oars to propel the craft across a lake or down a river. They're not recommended for intense whitewater, but they will handle some swells. As well, the fisherman can kick with his feet or simply stand up in a shallow spot. These little boats cost between $500 and $1,000.

There are new inventions every day. A fellow in the Roaring Fork Valley by the name of Butch Zigurs pioneered a new kind of fishing craft made by affixing a rowing platform and angler's chair to twin kayak hulls. They call it a Bi-yak. It will only hold one rower and one caster, but it will slip over even the shallowest riffles. For big water, they're too small and limited, but for small, rocky rivers, they're a great fishing craft.

There are dozens of methods of catching fish with a fly rod. John has also devised a way to troll with his fly rod from a river kayak while paddling.

Canoes

Of course, there is the traditional fishing craft for lakes, ponds, and slow rivers, and that's the canoe. Lake canoes and river canoes have a different design, however, and we don't recommend lake fishing in a river canoe. They're too tippy. Casting from a canoe is more difficult than other boats, because every movement causes a wiggle in the boat, and your seat is fairly low to the water. However, canoes are a great way to bring friends and family along, and what a wonderful way to see the outdoors. If you've never learned to paddle a canoe, it's helpful to know that the paddler in the rear of the boat can use his paddle as a rudder to steer the boat, and there are various strokes that help keep the course of the boat straight.

Flats Boats

If you venture into the world of saltwater flyfishing, you'll find yourself in a flats boat. Saltwater species such as tarpon, bonefish and bonita are found in shallow flats off tropical coastlines and islands. The guides propel their boats by small outboards or by pushing the boat, and the caster can stand up in the flat-bottomed boats to cast. Usually there is just one angler per guide. The guides are very adept at spotting quick-moving fish, and it's essential to make long, quick, accurate casts, often in strong winds, in order to be successful.

We love to wade fish. We love the challenge of spotting fish, making a good drift, seeing a strike and setting the hook, then playing the fish to the net. There's something very intellectually stimulating about reading the water and working your way up the river, casting to new and different fish over the course of an evening.

But for sheer excitement, there's nothing like floating a big, wild river on a drift boat during a prolific hatch, the light glimmering on the water from the sun going down in the west, and a new trout sucking in your fly every couple of minutes. After you get good enough to cast accurately, you ought to try it.

Guides

by Gary Hubbell

Chances are if you do much flyfishing, at one point or another, you'll be fishing with a guide. What makes a good guide? That's a very good question.

After guiding on my own for over ten years, I managed the guide service for the Ritz-Carlton Hotel in Aspen in 1997. I trained 11 new guides, supervised 700 fishing trips, and guided 170 trips personally that year. We had a list of over 25 qualified guides that we booked on a regular basis, and I know personally about 50 fishing guides.

First you have to understand that most guides are freelancers. They're free spirits, doing their own thing on their own schedules, and some of them may guide for several different outfitters in their local area. It all comes down to an accounting question—who's paying his Social Security taxes? If he's a full-time employee, the guide service will be pitching in for half of his Social Security taxes. If the guide gets a 1099 at the end of the year, that means he's an independent contractor, and he can work for whomever he wants. He can come and go as he pleases, and he can take a trip or decline it.

That means if you're a pain, he'll be busy next time you call to book a trip. You'll never fish with that guide again. A good guide, you see, is a psychologist, a counselor, an expert entomologist, a patient instructor, a jokester, a buddy, a good driver and a great fisherman. He is not guiding for the money—he's guiding because he loves knowing what's going on and he loves being outdoors. A good guide is the kind of person who can't stand it if he doesn't know whether or not the green drakes are hatching. He doesn't have time for people who are a pain in the butt.

Most guides are very intelligent people. They have inquisitive minds. They're great at noticing what is happening and then applying their observations to the situation at hand. A good guide can tell when you're getting hungry, when you're starting to get frustrated, when your marriage is in trouble, and when the hatch is going to start. An excellent guide will know these things before you know them yourself. He'll suggest lunch, leave you to fish on your own, take your wife to the side and pay attention to her, and change your pattern before you even realize what's happening. If he were to take his intelligence, analytical skills and people skills to the business world, he'd be making a six-figure salary in short order.

A good guide will instinctively know whether or not he can tell a dirty joke. He'll know if he can take you into a physically demanding spot and he'll know that you'll enjoy it. He'll also be able to tell if you're in poor shape and then he'll take you to the easiest spot on the river. However, you won't catch nearly as many fish. If you listen well, never complain and have a happy attitude, he will break his back for you. If you whine and bitch, he'll shut off inside and go through the motions until he can dump you off at the shop, because you obviously don't deserve to know how to flyfish.

A good guide will never offend you, but he might let you know if he disapproves of your politics or your occupation. He will not subject you to foul language, whiskey breath or cigarette smoke, or bore you with his divorce proceedings. A good guide will not try to sell you time-share real estate or trips to Mexico. He will snag the cigarette butt that you drop into the river without comment. If you do it twice, he will cuss you out. You will release your fish, even if the local regulations say you can keep them. He will be polite to other fishermen and he'll gladly share information. His appearance will be neat. In turn, you will show up on time and you will not step on a rod.

He is boss, but a good guide will make suggestions rather than bark orders. If you're not doing it right, he will not cuss you out. He will try to find another way to explain it to you. Listen to him. He is the expert. If he brings his Labrador, don't question it. The dog will be well behaved and will not ruin the fishing. He will have a cooler full of cold drinks. His box will be full of flies. His vest will be worn and his waders will be patched. He will know everybody in town. His vehicle will likely not be clean, though he tries. He leaves the keys in it.

The guide is there to give you good service, but he's not your servant. There's a difference. Do things for yourself if you can. If you're looking for a gourmet meal on the riverbank, then make your own arrangements with a catering service. He's a guide—not a chef. You can, however, let him know what you want on your sandwich.

Realize that the day isn't just about fishing. It doesn't matter how many you catch—or don't catch. See if you can learn something about the water ouzels, the local elk herd, or the bear population.

You can ask for your money back if: the guide makes an offensive joke about your ethnicity; the guide behaves poorly around other fishermen; the dog ruins the fishing; he screams at your kid. However, don't book a trip, make up something you don't like and then think it's good sport to beat the guide service down on price after the trip's over—that's a city game that guides don't play. Tips? Yes, for good service, $20 is minimal and $100 is greatly appreciated for great service on a half-day or full-day trip. Reach to the hip for more if it's a longer excursion. And lastly, don't be at all surprised if your guide is a "she." There are some great women guides on the rivers.

Some people question the value of hiring a guide, and to that I say "Where else can you find an ultimate professional to work so cheap?" An average to good lawyer costs $250 an hour, while a good guide makes that in a day. A decent plumber makes at least $50 an hour, and all he has to know is that stink goes up and...well, you know the rest. Think about this—what is your free time worth? How many days a year do you get to go flyfishing? And one more thing: you'll learn more in one day with a good guide that you'd learn fishing for three weeks on your own. You might even make a good friend in the process.

Chuck Fothergill, the consummate sportsman

Chapter Fourteen
Philosophy & Ethics

*B*y its very nature, flyfishing is a private pursuit. At its best, time spent flyfishing is a time of reflection and solace, when you can sort out your thoughts, clear your mind and refresh yourself. Whether you're alone or with a good friend or two doesn't seem to matter. You come away from the river feeling re-energized, happy and full of life. But it's possible to ruin a good time on the water, and that's why the sport has a strong sense of ethics.

There are some "rules," so to speak, that flyfishermen learn from one another, and the last thing you want to be is the person who violates these rules without even knowing it. First of all, you must understand the very basic concept that rivers flow downstream, fish look upstream, and flyfishermen work their way upstream. The water that they have waded through on their way upstream is considered disturbed. There is little sense in going downstream to fish water that has been muddied and the fish spooked away. Few fishermen will mind if you start fishing a few dozen yards below him, but expect his full wrath if you begin fishing a few yards upstream of him. That's his space where he is intending to fish next, and it's extremely poor form to violate that space. Even worse is to start upstream and move downstream into an area that someone is fishing, because not only have you intruded, you've also ruined the fishing while you're at it.

Space

In flyfishing, the sense of space is paramount, and you must be careful to respect it. And, one must remember that one person's sense of space can be far different from another's. For people who have grown used to rural, isolated surroundings, their personal borders are likely far greater than someone from a crowded city. That perspective translates directly to flyfishing. Though a half mile of river with two fishermen may seem practically deserted to someone from Manhattan, if those two fishermen are from Montana they might be highly offended if the New Yorker jumps right in to join the fun. On other rivers, the scale may be diminished greatly by the popularity of the fishing to be found there. On the San Juan or the Green, you may have trouble finding a hole that doesn't have three or four fishermen crowded into it. The parameters and expectations change with the popularity of the rivers.

Still, make no assumptions. If someone is fishing nearby, it's always good form to deliver a brief greeting, and then say something like, "Listen, I want to be sure to give you enough room to fish upstream. Would it be alright with you if I started by that big boulder up there?" The answer will likely be a polite, "Sure, go ahead," and if the fisherman isn't satisfied with your idea, he'll offer an alternative. It is lamentable to see grown-ups racing each other to the river to see who can hog a hole for the longest period of time. We've actually seen guides who, when guiding two clients, take one fisherman at a time over to the bank for lunch so that the other fisherman can stay in the hole and keep their spot. That's pitiful etiquette. If you've been fishing in a hole for more than an hour or two and other anglers are around, it's time to share.

Private Property

Some of the best fishing, it is well known, can be found on private waters. Though some folks hold to the concept that rivers and lakes should be the public domain for everyone to fish, it remains the law in some states and provinces that the property under the river or lake may belong to private individuals and they may protect the right to trespass. It is your responsibility to educate yourself as to the local rules and regulations regarding access. It is not the landowner's responsibility to catch you trespassing and confront you. These situations can become very unpleasant very quickly, and the sheriff might be called to find out who's right and who's wrong. Trespassing is a criminal offense, and we've seen people end up with a blot on their record from fishing without asking.

A more pleasant solution is to find out who owns a particular property and request permission to fish there, and explaining your catch-and-release ethic is always helpful in obtaining permission. Maybe an afternoon of helping fix fence or pruning the raspberries will win over a landowner, or perhaps a bottle of good wine or a special kind of chocolate could wave the magic wand. Who knows, you might end up making a good friend in the process. Another alternative that is becoming very popular is leasing property and charging anglers a daily rod fee, and who can argue? Agriculture is fast becoming a losing proposition, and the landowner who makes a few bucks from fishermen might keep his hay meadows from becoming another damned golf course.

Etiquette

We've made some good friends on the river, but don't assume that everyone you meet is in the mood to chat. They might have their own thoughts to hold onto, and a talkative stranger might be considered intrusive. As we said, a simple greeting is always appropriate. Some anglers are put off by the question "What are you using?" Personally, we don't mind sharing this information, but some folks take the position that, 'Hey, it took me quite a while to figure out how to learn to flyfish and that just might be my little secret that I don't feel like sharing, so go figure it out yourself.' That is not a particularly friendly attitude, but it exists, so don't expect everyone to be completely open to your questions. Also be aware that some anglers will be happy to lie about the fly they're using, frustrating you even further.

Flyfishing is a very clean sport, and of course littering is a huge transgression of the etiquette. Cigarette butts are litter. Throwing butts in the water will likely earn you a stern lecture from someone. Used strike indicators are litter, and so is a wad of used monofilament. Orange peels and banana peels, though biodegradable, do not belong in a river environment. If you must relieve yourself, do it as far away from the stream as possible, and human waste and toilet paper must be buried eight inches deep at least 100 feet from streamside. Aside from the obvious ethic of not littering, flyfishermen expect each other to clean up after those who do not possess this same sense of cleanliness. We've pulled real estate signs, bicycles, raft paddles, tennis balls, styrofoam coolers, tennis shoes, tires and barbed wire, to name a few items, from our favorite rivers, and generally a river that is visited by flyfishermen is a very clean river. And by the way, flyfishermen don't appreciate golfers who think it's cute to smack balls into the river.

Spawning

When it comes to the trout that we enjoy so much, there is a definite ethic as to their handling. First and foremost, it is well known among flyfishermen when certain species of fish spawn. Rainbow trout prefer the spring, cutthroats in the spring and summer, and German browns and brook trout in the fall. As we stated in Chapter 5, fishing over spawning trout is intolerable. If you insist on trying to catch them while they're spawning, the stress might void the process entirely, so that we lose a part of a future generation of trout. This isn't to say that you shouldn't fish at all while the trout are spawning. We fish year 'round. But there are obvious spots that fish inhabit when it's time to reproduce (usually shallow, rapid water with small-diameter gravel), and those spots should be avoided during spawning seasons. By the same token, the eggs take roughly 70 days to hatch, and walking through a redd during that time will crush them.

The San Juan Shuffle

Speaking of walking, we've noted how successful one can be at nymphing, because the fish feed so heavily on these immature underwater insects. It doesn't take much thought to figure out that, if you shuffle your feet on the bottom of the river, many nymphs will become dislodged and will float downstream to the waiting trout with a sort of chumming effect. The fish begin to feed heavily on the new food source, and if an artificial fly is inserted into the mixture, there's a good chance of hooking a fish. This practice is called the "San Juan Shuffle," and it's bad news. There's nothing sporting about it, and it destroys future generations of insects for a short-term thrill of catching a fish. Don't even think about stimulating your fishing with a "San Juan Shuffle" and a downstream cast. In fact, some states are even considering enacting laws against it, so not only is it unethical, it may be illegal.

The Natural Environment

Along the same lines, it should be your goal to enjoy the fishing environment as it is, not as you think it should be. Maybe a particular branch is in your way and inhibits your cast, but that doesn't mean you should tear it down. That branch might be the challenge that motivates you to become a better caster. On a greater scale, as man has discovered the power of machinery, it has become more and more tempting to alter a natural environment to a fishing ideal. Like plastic surgery, some of these attempts are better than others. Rows of boulders placed in a stream may provide an obvious place to cast, but do they really provide fish habitat? Or do they provide "fisherman habitat?" "Stream improvements" is the buzzword of real estate agents and developers to sell riverfront property, but should you be fortunate enough to influence what happens to a piece of riverfront, keep in mind that nature has a way of making her wishes known, and she's been in the river business much longer than we have. As well, accomplishing stream improvements requires a permit from the U.S. Army Corps of Engineers, and if you're caught moving rocks around in a river without it, you may find yourself in very big trouble with the federal government.

As you learn to flyfish, you'll evolve along a rough pattern of proficiency and expectations in the sport. In the beginning, you'll be challenged by the newness of it all, and it will be a great success to master the basics: rigging the rod, selecting a fly, casting, and finally setting the hook and catching a fish. As you become more skillful, you'll find other things to be important. You'll want to catch more fish, and bigger fish. A certain amount of well-deserved boasting will accompany this phase. Then you'll find, as you get better at it, that catching a lot of fish isn't as important as finding a good challenge, like catching a selective fish on a size 22 fly, or catching a trout on a fly you've tied yourself. Or maybe the trick is to catch a trout in a tiny, brushy stream where casting is difficult and the fish are spooky.

Eventually, if you stick with it long enough, you'll find that the satisfaction lies in more subtle things, like a good cast, the dog that swam the river to come with you, the beaver that almost swam between your legs, or the chuckle you get watching the baby ducks try to fly for the first time.

We implore you not to get stuck in the second phase. Don't let your fishing ego get in the way of a good day of being outdoors. For example, we were driving back with our partner Paul from fishing the Bighorn River in Montana and stopped off to see Yellowstone National Park. Two fellows were fishing the Firehole River with a herd of bison in the background. When the bison started to cross the river, we were thrilled at the sight. Forty head of buffalo swimming the river at once! Wow! How many people have seen that in person? Yet the fishermen (who weren't catching anything, anyway) were visibly disgusted at the interruption.

Don't let the process of fishing overcome the joy of being outdoors. Fishing braggarts are boring. Please resist the urge to quantify everything. Rare is the day when we count how many fish we catch. Neither of us know how far we can cast. We have no idea how many days we fished this year, or how many rivers we've fished. We won't bore you with how much our equipment is worth or how many rods we have. Instead, we remember the moments, fish, places, rivers, people, weather, roads, rods, guides, dogs, flies, restaurants, vehicles, and much more. There are some things that stand out from the others like a racehorse ahead of the pack. We remember the trout that jumped and hovered in the air for an impossibly long time before falling back into the river, the red-tailed hawk that flew overhead with the writhing snake in his talons, the time the dog almost caught the goose swimming in the main current of the river, the time we didn't catch a thing, but collected twenty flies off the bushes on the far side of the stream. But as the years go by, nobody will care about numbers: how far you can cast, how many fish you caught, how few flies you lost, how much, how much, how much...ad nauseum.

If it seems as if we have a high-minded approach to the sport, we don't mind that label. We both grew up fishing from childhood, and the sport means as much to us as our homes and our families. One phenomenon that we have noticed, as guides and fishing professionals, is that some people who learn the sport later in life have had no role models to teach them acceptable etiquette. Certain practices may be acceptable in the cutthroat world of business or stressful city life, but those same practices do not play well on a trout stream. Something is missing, something that checks the ego. We think that "something" is the tradition handed down to an adolescent or a child by a father, an uncle, or a favorite family friend.

So we find ourselves in the somewhat uncomfortable position of providing a role model to folks who might be our seniors in any other walk of life. So be it. Just recognize that we've been on the water for many, many days of flyfishing, and we've spent many more days thinking about what the sport means to us. We do not impart our thoughts lightly. And, you might question our motives in writing this book. Are we exploiting our knowledge of the rivers and the trout in them to make a buck selling books? In all honesty, maybe a little. We all have to make a living somehow. But we've seen many folks gain a greater appreciation of nature through flyfishing, and we'd like to think we've made a difference in people's lives.

More than that, we know that if people come to love nature, they will also fight to protect nature. If we can help you find a little peace and harmony in your life through flyfishing, we welcome you to the sport. While you're at it, be sure to let your elected representatives and government officials know your feelings on protecting rivers and wild areas. We wish you peace, and *tight lines*!

A Fond Farewell
to Chuck Fothergill

by Gary Hubbell

Among those of us who work in the flyfishing industry, there are all kinds of characters with all kinds of flaws. There are those of us with hot tempers, drinking problems, golf addictions, the fishing guide braggart's syndrome, greedy merchant's syndrome, and liars who will do anything to book a trip. It's a small world, prone to vicious rumors and the occasional fistfight.

However, there are some individuals in the world of flyfishing who stand out as a shining example to us all, people who seem to exemplify the wonderful ideals of the sport. Chuck Fothergill was one of those people. His was a world of kindness, appreciation, wry humor, generosity, and the highest ethics of the true sportsman. I particularly remember a letter he wrote to the editor of the local newspaper, chiding a group of guides who had gotten into the habit of bringing their unsuspecting clients to spawning redds to fish over spawning trout. Anything for a hook-up, I guess. Anything for a tip. While he definitely made his point that he thought those guides were lower than pond scum, he made his point in such a gentlemanly fashion that it seemed like he'd be having them all over for dinner that night.

Chuck enjoyed a stellar reputation in an industry where jealousy and pettiness can sometimes get the better of us. Chuck was an innovator in the sport—the author of several good guidebooks, the inventor of the fly vest, a respected outfitter, and one of the flyfishermen responsible for defining the now-classic nymphing technique. He was loved by all.

I knew Chuck hadn't been feeling well, because I called him up to guide a trip for us in April of 1996. His back was bothering him something fierce, and he declined the trip, which was uncharacteristic for Chuck. I knew Chuck had defeated cancer once, but back problems didn't sound related. But a scant couple of months later, Chuck passed away from a recurrence of prostate cancer while I was on an extended fishing trip to Montana. I was very sad, and I thought about him often.

On a sunny day in early June, the river was clearing from the spring runoff, the hatches were starting, and I was thinking about going fishing, but I wanted to check the mail first. I was startled when I reached into the mailbox, because one of the letters bore the return address of Chuck Fothergill. I was surprised, to say the least.

The black type burned from the page in the bright early-summer sun. It read,

"Dear Friends,
I'm writing this letter to advise you that I will most likely perish from cancer within a few weeks.

There is also some very good news! Paula and I were married on a bright, sunny Saturday morning. We had often thought of marriage but always said, 'When the time is right, we can do it.' The time now seemed conspicuously right and we enjoyed a small ceremony.

One positive note to all this is the fact that someday—strictly on your schedule—we'll meet again along the banks of that beautiful river on the other side. I'll scout it out before you get there, and we'll take turns working each riffle and pool.

I've been very fortunate—I've lived a great life.
                              Love,
                              Chuck"

I stood there in the bright summer sun by the mailbox, and the words on the page started swimming as my eyes filled with tears. Even in death, Chuck remained so dignified, compassionate and caring. He passed with grace and charm, like the true gentleman that he was. My respect for Chuck, always profound, became even deeper. I stood there in the driveway and bawled like a baby. I miss him still.

Glossary

Action - The act of dragging a fly across the current and giving it an unnatural drift.

Adam's Special - A general, widely-used dry fly pattern to imitate an adult mayfly.

Adult - The final phase of an insect's life cycle, most often occurring above water for aquatic insects.

Attractor patterns - Bright, bold flies that do not imitate any insect in particular, but many insects in general. Attractor patterns often provoke a trout's tendency to strike.

Backing - Thin, strong string that is attached to a fly reel to fill up the spool before attaching the fly line.

Baetis - A small grey mayfly.

Blood knot - A knot used to tie two pieces of tippet together - also known as a barrel knot.

Brook trout - Actually a member of the char family, brook trout are often small in size and populate small streams. Brook trout have a greenish body with "squiggly" markings, orange and black spots, and orange fins with a white stripe on the anterior side.

Caddis - A general name for the dozens of subspecies of caddis flies found in trout streams all over the world. Also known as a "sedge," they are characterized by a tent-like wing. Caddis have four stages of development, from egg to larva to pupa to adult.

Catch and release - The ethic of returning a trout or other fish to the water unharmed.

Cover - A place for a trout to rest in relative security from predators and current.

Cuttbow - A rainbow/cutthroat hybrid, the cuttbow has both the rainbow's stripe and a cutthroat's "slash" under its jaw.

Cutthroat trout - A native to many Rocky Mountain rivers, the cutthroat has a crimson "slash" under its jaw and black spots concentrated near the tail.

Dead drift - A drift that imitates the natural action of an insect by floating directly downstream with the current.

Downstream drift - The act of allowing the fly to drift past the fisherman and rise to the surface on the river below him, particularly on a nymph drift.

Drag - When a fly line catches on a current, making the fly drift in an unnatural fashion. Also the mechanical device on a fly reel that limits how fast a fish can strip line from the reel.

Drift boat - Also known as a Mackenzie river dory, it's a river fishing craft ranging between 14 and 18 feet long with a flat bottom, upswept prow and rigid hull.

Dropper - The secondary fly tied on the end of the leader after the lead fly.

Dry fly - A pattern designed to imitate an adult insect, floating on top of the water.

Dubbing - A wrapping to thicken the body of a fly, made by rubbing ground-up muskrat fur, rabbit fur or other substance onto a waxed thread.

Eddy - A calm spot next to a fast current, or in the case of a "back eddy," where the current switches direction.

Emerger - An insect in the transition period from hatching off the bottom of the river to flying away from the surface of the water as an adult insect.

Evening hatch - When many insects choose to emerge from under the water.

False casting - Casting ever-increasing segments of line, or casting the same amount of line, keeping the line aloft in the air without touching the water.

Flats - A place where water is still and shallow. Trout generally use flats only for feeding purposes because they feel vulnerable there.

Flyfisherman (or, politically correct, "flyfisher") A person of either gender who pursues the sport of flyfishing.

Flies - Artificial imitations of the aquatic and terrestrial insects found in and near trout streams. Flies are tied of many and various materials, such as feathers, fur, thread, tinsel, and even space-age materials. Patterns imitating minnows, baitfish and other fish and crustacean species are also called "flies."

Float tube - A one-man fishing flotation device for lake and slow river fishing that looks like an inner tube covered with a cloth mesh liner, seat, and back rest.

Floatant - A coating designed to keep a dry fly from becoming waterlogged.

Fry - Baby trout

German brown trout - A native of the European continent, the brown trout has a golden sheen and black and orange speckles with white rings around them.

Green Drake - A large, green-bodied mayfly found in many trout streams, a particular favorite food for trout.

Hackle - The series of extended fibers right behind the eye of a fly. The hackle is what allows a dry fly to float.

High-sticking - Holding the rod high to keep the line taut in a nymphing drift.

Improved clinch knot - The suggested knot for tying a fly to the leader or tippet.

Indicator species - A species of plants or animals that suffers when pollution or environmental stress begins, thus indicating environmental degradation.

Jacobson Downdrift - Feeding slack into the line as the fly emerges downstream to imitate an emerging insect. Also known as a "back drift.

Larva - The second, or "worm" phase of an insect's life cycle.

Lead fly - The primary fly tied on the end of a fly line.

Leader - The piece of clear, tapered monofilament line attached to the fly line, usually between six and 15 feet long.

Leading - *(pronounced "leeding")* The act of keeping the rod tip and strike indicator downstream of the drifting nymph.

Leech - A bloodsucking worm that trout love to eat.

Line weight - The relative weight of the line. A "1 weight" rod is very light, while a "14 weight" rod is very heavy and throws large flies.

Loop - The candy-cane pattern made by a fly line as it is cast. The tighter the loop, the more accurate and powerful the cast.

Matching the hatch - Choosing the fly pattern that imitates the insects that are hatching nearby.

Mayfly - The most beautiful of aquatic insects, the mayfly is characterized by an upswept wing and long, delicate two- or three-stranded tail. The mayfly goes through three stages—egg, nymph, and adult—then metamorphoses once again from a sub-imago adult to a spinner.

Mending - The act of lifting the fly line off the water and flipping it either upstream or downstream to eliminate drag and accomplish a more natural drift.

Merging currents - A dead spot of calm water created where two currents come together.

Midge - A very small species of aquatic insects found in trout streams. Many species of midges hatch into adults in the middle of winter. They have four stages of development, from egg to larva to pupa to adult.

Minnow - A small fish, usually a baitfish.

Nail knot - The knot used to attach a leader to the fly line or to the butt section.

Nymph phase - The immature phase of an aquatic insect's life cycle that occurs underwater.

Overhand cast - A nymphing cast where the fisherman rotates the rod directly overhand while casting.

Phytoplankton - Macroscopic "buglike" creatures, smaller than the head of a pin, that are found in rivers and lakes.

Pocket water - Where fast current rushes around boulders and other obstructions, creating pockets of calmer water.

Polarized glasses - A very necessary part of a flyfisherman's kit. By virtue of a "grille" of tiny bars sandwiched between two layers of glass, polarized glasses eliminate glare reflected from water and allow a fisherman to see into the water.

Pool - A deep, slow hole.

Pupa - The third phase of an insect's life cycle, when wings are beginning to grow.

Rainbow trout - A beautiful trout species characterized by a brilliant pink stripe running lengthways down its side. The rainbow is a silvery fish and has black spots.

Reach cast - A cast with a built-in mend accomplished by extending the arm and placing the line upstream or downstream of where it would have landed with a normal cast.

Redd - A spawning bed for trout, identifiable by a hollow of clean gravel in a mild current.

Retrieval - The act of bringing in slack line (also called "stripping" by many flyfishermen.)

Reverse cast - The nymphing cast made by casting across the body on the "off" hand side of the stream. (For a right-handed fisherman, the right side of the stream. For a left-handed fisherman, the left bank.) Also called the "Western roll cast."

Riffle - Where the current rolls over a rocky bar and then slows down.

Rigging - The process of preparing a rod to flyfish.

Rod - The thin, strong stick made of graphite, fiberglass, bamboo or steel used to cast a fly line and play a fish.

Run - A smooth, deep glide of water that usually follows a riffle.

Sculpin - An ugly little fish found in trout streams that trout love to eat.

Seam - A calm spot caused by an obstruction in a river such as a rock or log, or where two currents meet.

"Spank equals spook" - Disturbing the water with an overly aggressive cast will spook the fish you hope to catch.

Spinner - The last phase of a mayfly's life, the spinner dances above the water until it mates and the female lays eggs, whereupon the spinners die.

Spinner fall - When mayfly spinners, after having successfully mated and laid their eggs, die en masse.

Spring runoff - The time of year when the snow melts and runs into the rivers, swelling the trout streams with a great volume of water.

Snelled flies - Old-fashioned flies that came attached with a short, thick leader with a loop knot.

Stonefly - One of the major species of aquatic insects found in a trout stream. Stoneflies have three phases of development, from egg to nymph to adult, and may live underwater as long as four years before hatching to an adult winged insect. Stonefly nymphs often crawl out of the river to hatch out of their nymphal shucks on rocks.

Streamer - A fly tied to resemble a leech, minnow or sculpin.

Strike - When a fish eats the fly.

Strike indicators - Little "bobbers" made of foam, cork or yarn that indicate when a fish has eaten the fly tied on the line below it by a change in movement and the drift.

Stripping - The act of retrieving slack very quickly, often with a motion designed to give action to a streamer or other fly.

Surgeon's knot - A knot used to tie two pieces of tippet together

Tailwater Fishery - a stream or river whose water originates from cold water that descends from the bottom of a dam, producing consistent temperatures for trout habitat year-round.

"Ten to two" - The casting motion whereby the position of the rod tip is compared to the hands of a clock.

Terrestrials - Insect species whose life cycle occurs on land, such as beetles and grasshoppers.

Thirty Second Rule - After 30 seconds out of the water, trout have little chance of surviving if released.

Thorax - The part of an artificial fly or real insect that relates to the "shoulders and chest" of a fly.

Tippet - Monofilament leader material that is the same diameter throughout. Tippet is measured from the very fine (7x) to the very heavy (0x).

Twist-on - A brand of lead weight that comes in strips like a matchbook.

Undercut bank - A dark holding spot for trout where current has gouged material out from under a riverbank.

Wing case - The structure on an aquatic insect or artificial nymph that holds the undeveloped wings on the back of the immature insect.